BLENDED, NOT SHAKEN

Support for Stepparrents

Ginny Schuyler Warren

Gotham Books

30 N Gould St.
Ste. 20820, Sheridan, WY 82801
https://gothambooksinc.com/

Phone: 1 (307) 464-7800

© 2023 *Ginny Schuyler Warren*. All rights reserved.

No part of this book may be reproduced, stored in a retrieval system, or transmitted by any means without the written permission of the author.

Published by Gotham Books (April 28, 2023)

ISBN: 979-8-88775-264-8 (P)
ISBN: 979-8-88775-265-5 (E)
ISBN: 979-8-88775-266-2 (H)

Because of the dynamic nature of the Internet, any web addresses or links contained in this book may have changed since publication and may no longer be valid.

The views expressed in this work are solely those of the author and do not necessarily reflect the views of the publisher, and the publisher hereby disclaims any responsibility for them.

Contents

Preface: A Redeemed Life vii

**Section 1 – Stepparenting Was Not Our Dream,
But Here We Are, Raising Other People's Children** 1

Chapter 1
Blended, Not Shaken 3

Chapter 2
You Are a Role Model Whether You Like It or Not 10

**Section 2 – What Issues Do We Face That Are
Unique to Us As Stepparents?** 17

Chapter 3
Challenges We Face 19

Chapter 4
Look, Jerk's Mom! 25

Chapter 5
Grace That's Yours 31

Chapter 6
The Basics of the Blended Family 37

Chapter 7
Exactly How Are We Related? 47

**Section 3 – What Do We Do Now As
We Move Forward?** 55

Chapter 8
Family Identity 57

Chapter 9
Things You Can Control: Thing One: Love Your Spouse
and Show Love to the Children..63

Chapter 10
Things You Can Control: Thing Two: Preserve Your
Life – Hold Your Tongue 71

Chapter 11
Things You Can Control: Thing Three: Enforce the Rules
of Your House 77

Chapter 12
Things You Can Control: Thing Four: Rely on God and Pray ...82

Chapter 13
Counting Noses 90

Chapter 14
That's Not Fair...95

Chapter 15
It's the Most Wonderful Time of the Year—or Is It?.................102

Chapter 16
A Picture-Perfect Family...108

Chapter 17
Extreme Circumstances... 115

Chapter 18
A Redeemed Life 124

Notes 133

Preface: A Redeemed Life

The complexity of relationships in blended families means that they face a unique set of difficulties. In these pages I will address these issues through Scripture and in light of my own experience in order to support stepparents in their roles and strengthen the blended family.

Years ago my husband, Steve, and I were asked to lead a breakout session for stepparents at a weekend parenting conference in Phoenix, Arizona. We accepted, and I set out to find some relevant books with which to lead the discussion. I found none. I even traveled to Colorado Springs and looked at Christian bookstores there, including Focus on the Family's extensive selection, and found nothing I could use. Eventually I found two books from the 1970s about the "rare" phenomenon of blending families to create one unit. That wasn't going to work, so I wrote my own material.

The breakout session at the parenting conference was energizing and informative. I realized then that this was a topic that needed to be addressed in the church. The blended families among us that weekend needed support. Many of the attendees desperately wanted to start a regular small group meeting to help them blend more smoothly. However, we were moving out of state and were not able to lead such a group at the time. I started thinking that maybe I could compile the material and write a book. The task was out of my realm of experience, but if it could help some families, I wanted to get it out there.

The process has met with many obstacles, from illness to family issues, work challenges, and the busyness of raising my youngest children. Church leaders told us stories of blended family groups failing and all the leaders ending up divorced. I had almost given up and soon found myself in tears about something totally unrelated to the book, praying, "God, what should I do?" I heard clearly, "Write your book." That wasn't even on my list of options, but it was undeniable that this was what I should do. So, here it is. There are Scriptures to hold onto, stories about our family, questions for group discussion, and bits of encouragement that I hope will help your family to be blended, not shaken.

I'd like to acknowledge and thank those who contributed directly and indirectly to the creation of this work: my sister, who listened to me read aloud the book in its entirety, giving me input and encouragement before submission; the pastors who cheered us on when we had our blended family group meeting at our home; my writing group, whose members helped me with wording and editing; and most of all, my family, who lived the life presented in these pages and have been willing to help others through their blended family experience.

Section 1

Stepparenting Was Not Our Dream, But Here We Are, Raising Other People's Children

Blended, Not Shaken

The basic elements for a successful marriage are the same in intact and blended families; they include such things as love, respect, communication, and the desire to give and to give some more. The difficulty in implementing these things and achieving success, however, implies that statistics do not favor the blended family. A successful marriage in such cases will take more effort and more grace, but it can be accomplished.

Success as I mean it here is not measured by the perfection of your parenting techniques or how wonderful your children are in the eyes of the world. Success depends on how you deal with the inevitable conflicts in your marriage and with your children and stepchildren. Success shows itself in your resolve to remain a family and in your willingness to share struggles, joys, friendship, and conflict in this journey through life.

In my experience, there are two helpful elements required for the success of the blended family. The first is the married couple's commitment to the marriage. Commitment is too easily tossed aside when the going gets tough. People tend to dismiss commitment because we are told that our happiness is more important than others'. We hear fancy explanations about improving our emotional health. "Get out and get healthy" is a phrase I have heard numerous times from women pursuing divorce. More often than not, if both spouses are willing to weather the storm and work on the marriage, they will accomplish success. Later I will discuss reasons to seek divorce, but first I want to encourage commitment to the marriage for the wellbeing of the family.

The second element that increases the chances of a successful blended family is a willingness to embrace God's Word as a guide. The Bible is full of truth that will breathe life into your marriage. You cannot control what other people do, but you can experience the peace that comes with knowing God and following his living Word.

The following Scripture speaks of the Lord on whom I rely to help me to raise my children. God's Word provides the encouragement I need in order to maneuver the tumultuous trials of being a member of a blended family: "My soul, wait in silence for God only, For my hope is from Him. He only is my rock and my salvation, My stronghold; I shall not be shaken. On God my salvation and my glory rest; The rock of my strength, my refuge is in God. Trust in Him at all times, O people; Pour out your heart before Him; God is a refuge for us" (Psalm 62:5–8 NASB).

Stepfamilies are not as rare today as they were when I was a child in the 1960s. I remember hearing from one of my first- or second-grade classmates that her parents were getting divorced. I was shocked. I didn't know anyone who had divorced parents, stepparents, or any other kind of "broken" or restructured family.

Following are some statistics on divorce and blended families in the United States compiled by Ron Deal, M.MFT.[1]

How Prevalent Are Stepfamilies?

- Among married couples with children in the United States, 40 percent are stepcouples (meaning at least one partner had a child from a previous relationship before marriage; this includes full- and part-time residential stepfamilies and

those with children under or over the age of eighteen). The percentage of *all* married couple households is 35 percent.[2]
- According to a demographic estimate by Ron Deal, approximately one-third of all weddings in the United States today form stepfamilies (demographic estimate, Deal). In 2001, 38 percent of all US marriages were remarriages for one or both partners (15 percent for both; 23 percent for one).[3]

A national report (Parker, 2011) by the Pew Research Center on adults in America updated our national statistics on stepfamilies for the first time in a decade. Note that these statistics apply only to adults and do not include children under eighteen years of age.[4]

- Step-relationships include approximately 42 percent of adults are a part of a stepfamily, either as a stepparent, a step- or half-sibling, or a stepchild. This translates to 95.5 million adults.
- Among all adults, 13 percent are stepparents (29 to 30 million); 15 percent of men are stepdads (16.5 million) and 12 percent of women are stepmoms (14 million).

Other notable statistics include the following items:

- There are 14 million stepmothers in the United States today (married or cohabiting). This statistic does not include stepmothers whose stepchildren are over eighteen.
- There are 35 million Americans in the United States today who are remarried. There are an additional 36 million Americans who are divorced or widowed (and will possibly find themselves in a remarriage at some point).[5]
- One-third of individuals who had been divorced before 2008 found themselves divorcing again.[6]
- Only about one-third of stepfamily marriages last until death parts the spouses. Approximately 60 percent of second

marriages end in divorce, as do approximately 73 percent of third marriages.[7]
- Serial transitions in and out of marriage, divorce, and cohabitation are now typical of family life in the United States, yielding significant consequences for children.[8]
- Americans marry, divorce, and cohabit at higher rates than in any other Western society. They also start and stop relationships more quickly.
- Children living with two married parents in the United States have a higher risk of experiencing a family breakup than do children living with two unmarried parents in Sweden.
- Among US women, 10 percent have had three or more marriages, divorces, or cohabiting partners by age thirty-five (the next highest percentage in an industrialized nation is Sweden at 4.5 percent).
- Among people born after 1970, 16 percent will marry, divorce, remarry, and redivorce.
- By age fifteen, 29 percent of US children have experienced two or more mother partnerships (either by marriage or cohabitation).
- The more parental partnerships (transitions in and out of couple relationships) that children experience, the lower will be their overall emotional, psychological, and academic well-being.

These statistics do not dictate how you will fare; they just point out that it is not always easy to stay married and that staying remarried is especially difficult. If you can be encouraged and empowered to stay married and raise your blended family by learning from my experience, then my purpose for this book will have been fulfilled. This book will discuss ways to provide a stable, warm, nurturing, and moral environment in which to raise your children.

Each chapter in this book has questions for contemplation and discussion. If you are reading this book with a group, you may not want to share all your answers with the whole group, and that is okay. Think about the questions and answers. Determine if they apply to you, whether you want to share your answers, and with whom you might share. As a guideline, you could ask yourself, "Will sharing help me? Will sharing hurt someone? Will sharing help someone other than me? Will keeping the answer to this question hidden allow something bad to happen or a situation to get worse?" Most things improve when they are discussed with someone trustworthy, but you don't need to air your dirty laundry to everyone. Keep group discussions confidential, unless someone is in danger.

Questions for Discussion

1. Are you in a blended family or considering entering into a blended family?

2. How long have you been married, or when do you plan to marry?

3. Do you have stepchildren? If so, describe your relationship.

4. What are the names, ages, and genders of your children and stepchildren?

5. What would you like to accomplish by reading this book or attending this group?

6. What brought you to this group?

7. What is your vision of how family life will look once you complete this study?

Notes

You Are a Role Model Whether You Like It or Not

When my sister, Kristin, and I were little girls playing make-believe, she would call out, "I'm the princess in *Around the World in Eighty Days*, long blue dress, puffed-up sleeves, and down!" *Down* referred to how the sleeves became fitted down the forearm. She had a very specific character she wanted to portray, a character who was cherished, valuable, and beautiful to someone who loved her.

Who among us is not aware that little girls commonly play at being a princess, bride, and mommy? It strikes me that these are the most common roles played, with princess thrown right into the happy mix. Girls also play many other roles while discovering their interests, such as doctor, veterinarian, and teacher, to name a few. But most girls start with the top three: princess, bride, and mommy.

Obviously children are familiar with mommy and bride, but why princess? How many of us personally know a princess? Disney may have something to do with it, but I think the underlying reason for girls to adopt this role is that from an early age we want to be loved, admired, and regarded as beautiful; we each want to be someone who is treasured.

Boys have their games too. Most involve battles, but the battles are never against the princess. They are against the baddies—monsters or dragons—and involve weapons, rules, and winning. The princess is usually protected by the boy or fighting alongside him in unity. He is strong, respected, and worthy of praise.

Have you ever seen children play divorce? I haven't. It's not something we dream about achieving in our future; we are much more idealistic than that. God designs each of us for oneness with a spouse, if we choose to marry. We don't dream of being widowed either, just as we don't dream of being dysfunctional or depressed.

Consider your home a training ground for future spouses. This book will discuss many ways to set a good example and model grace as a spouse. It is important to speak to your children about your commitment to your spouse. Help them see that your commitment exists even when you are feeling grumpy, angry, or sad and even when you are just not that excited for the time being with your life or marriage.

What we model for the children in our charge will stick with them into their adult lives. When you begin your new marriage, you may fall into some of the old patterns that contributed to the demise of your first marriage. You might exhibit behaviors that are a result of past hurts, such as defensiveness, fear of speaking up, or codependency. You may have low self-esteem. You may lash out in anger or live in fear of being hurt again. There was a time, several years into my second marriage, when I realized I was still guarded in an unhealthy way. I had a bit of a figurative wall to keep my husband, Steve, at a distance in order to protect myself from being deeply hurt again. The thing that I used to protect myself actually prevented me from experiencing the closeness I could have in our relationship.

This realization came to me after I had lunch with a close friend who had found out her husband was having an affair. While we talked that day she asked me what she could have done differently that might have prevented his affair, and she asked if I thought she was pretty. I ached for her broken heart.

When I got home I looked in the mirror and said to myself, "I will never be hurt like that again." Until that moment I hadn't realized that I was still holding Steve at a distance in order to protect myself. I envisioned in front of me a rock wall that had been knocked down to about mid-shin level. There was still a little bit of a wall and the rubble at my feet keeping me from the closeness I really wanted but was afraid to allow. Once I knew it was there, I took action to kick it down. I acknowledged that it existed, and I refused to keep myself closed off and distant from Steve. I talked about it and prayed about it. The freedom I gained immediately improved my relationship.

Although it may not come naturally to you, you can learn, as I did, to develop new patterns. You can make those patterns into habits that become second nature. Be purposeful in developing healthy habits and thought patterns. It will take practice. Take an honest look at yourself, take note of your shortcomings, and do what you need to do to overcome them.

It is natural to fear repeating unhealthy patterns that would be detrimental to your new marriage. Open communication with your spouse about your fears is important, and professional counseling is sometimes very helpful in recognizing the fears and changing those negative patterns of behavior. Once you recognize them, it is easier to move on.

Realize and accept that you are not perfect. Your kids already know this about you. They may have pointed it out to you on occasion. My daughters reminisce about things I did or didn't do. They launch into hilarious accounts of their childhood, each in her own style and exaggerated flair. For example, I have been reminded of the time I took adorable pictures of them having fun in the countryside, Whitney with flowers tucked into the top of her overalls. The subsequent rash and itching were not so adorable or fun. This is a minor event in a long string of parenting decisions, good and not so good, but we stuck it out together.

The way your children and stepchildren see you work through problems and stick to your commitments will help them do the same. Be humble, seek forgiveness when necessary, and be willing to laugh at yourself. Train them to be dedicated spouses who will be committed to their families, and empower them to break the chain of divorce in your family. Remember the deeper meanings of your childhood games. Foster the sweet dreams of your children, dreams of being valuable, cherished, respected, lovely, and strong. Teach them to bestow those values on their future spouses. I don't want my little ones to play divorce. Do you?

Questions for Discussion

1. Do you remember a specific role-playing game you played as a child? Talk about it and how it lines up with your dreams today.

2. What are some good examples you have set for your children and stepchildren?

3. Do you have any fears associated with repeating negative behaviors from your past?

4. How do your children imitate you in their play?

5. What would you like to change in yourself to be a better role model?

6. How will you make the changes you desire?

7. What are some things you have already accomplished toward achieving a healthy relationship with your spouse?

8. Have you moved on, or are you still living as a victim? Do you have a bit of a wall of protection between you and your spouse?

Notes

Section 2

What Issues Do We Face That Are Unique to Us As Stepparents?

Challenges We Face

My life did not end up at all like the fairy tale game I played as a child. My first marriage produced two wonderful children and a multitude of agonizing wounds. After dating for eight years and being married for six and a half years, my ex-husband and I separated and eventually were divorced. It was a difficult time, but it was also a time of growth for me.

A few years after I became a single mom, I came to the knowledge that I didn't need a husband to feel complete. I was just fine raising my children and relying on Jesus for the rest of my life. That was when I met Steve in the doorway to our daughters' two adjoining Sunday school classrooms at church. He was a single dad with a daughter between the ages of my two children. It was a few months before we went on our first date because our schedules were tight and God was still working on me. We enjoyed a short time of dating, counseled with our pastor, and got engaged.

Steve and I married on April 11, 1992, about a year after we first met on that fateful Sunday school threshold. Our children participated in our wedding. At the time friends asked me if we planned to have more children, and my honest response was, "No. We already have three."

We had three "ping-pong kids," a term my friend Carol used to refer to children who traveled back and forth between their parents' different homes. She had several ping-pong grandchildren of her own. For ease of communication, I employ the term in this text.

The ping-pong kids were my son, Cameron, who was eight at the time of our wedding; my daughter, Whitney, who was almost five; and Steve's daughter, Samantha, who was six.

A month into the marriage, I began to think about how great it would be to have children with Steve. He is a real family man, attentive to our children, and I longed to raise a baby (or two) with such a terrific father. Two years later, in May 1994, our son Stefan was born; seventeen months following him Eric, made his entrance. This gave us a family of five children ranging in age from newborn Eric to twelve-year-old Cameron.

As the children grew up, Samantha spent her weeks living in two houses, her mother's and ours. Cameron and Whitney had some time with their dad, Bob, and his parents. The little boys, Stefan and Eric, stayed with us and watched the revolving door as their older half-siblings came and went.

Now that our stepchildren are grown and gone, Steve and I reflect on the years raising the ping-pong kids with the broad perspective of people who have been there and done that. We did some things well and some not so well, and we learned a lot by trial and error. None of our friends shared our blended family configuration. My friend Carol, whom I mentioned above, was a widow married to a widower, so their brood of six children had no other parents to visit. Although they had all suffered a great loss, they had no other homes to deal with. Carol and her husband were my parents' age and had no children left at home when Steve and I married. With no blended families our age to befriend, Steve and I felt quite alone as we muddled through our children's formative years.

We attended parenting groups with intact couples and family camps with our church, also comprised of mostly intact families. We learned a lot and had general support, but when it came to the unique issues faced by stepparents, we had nothing. I can't tell you how many times I heard, "I've never been divorced, so I can't relate to what you are going through at all."

With God's grace and wisdom and our perseverance, we managed to get through those years. The thing that had the biggest impact on our family's success was that we serve a faithful God. Through all our tough times, we followed the Lord. Mistakes were made and conflicts occurred, but God is good and draws us and our children close no matter how many times we blow it. Some of our children have thanked us for sticking to our values during the times they opposed us. Those were tough days, but I am happy to see that the battle for our children's hearts was worth the effort. Now, all in their twenties and thirties, our ping-pong kids have grown to be responsible, caring adults.

Our adult children do not always do things our way or think the way we do, but they are all making their ways in life. When they were young, our foremost goal was not for them to like us or to behave in a certain way; it was for their hearts, which would serve them either in constructive or destructive ways for the rest of their lives, to be pure. And now they are our mature and wise friends. We enjoy their company, ask their opinions on important topics, and trust their judgment. They are also now good parents themselves.

I recently began a battle with breast cancer. As soon as my children found out, they came to my side. At that time Stefan and Eric still lived at home. Samantha and her family lived here in town, Cameron lived out of state, and Whitney lived out of the country with her family. Before my surgery, they all came to be with me and support me. Whitney brought her baby girl, and Cameron brought his girlfriend. It was fun to have them here, and it took my mind off of the heavy diagnosis and upcoming treatments.

Whitney sat in on doctors' appointments with Steve and me. She helped me sort through the enormous amount of information I was getting from surgeons and oncologists and make decisions about treatment. Steve took time off of work, but Whitney was able to stay and care for me when he went back. She knew what to do because of her experience as an EMT working in a hospital, and because she knows me. She was able to anticipate my needs so that I rarely had to ask for anything.

All my kids encouraged me in their own way. To top it off, Eric, who was graduating from high school, had me cap him at his capping ceremony two weeks after my first surgery. His quote was read as we took the stage: "My mom has been through a lot recently … I hope she is as proud of me as I am of her." I am so proud of my children.

Proverbs 31:28 says, "Her children arise and call her blessed" (NIV). This is what my children did for me by caring for me during that difficult time; they encouraged me and gave me strength.

We are a family who struggles with the kinds of issues that all families face. Like you, we weather trials and live our lives with all the pain and uncertainty inherent in human life. There is no formula for every family or every child, but I can say with certainty that there is never a valid reason to dismiss your values in order to get your child's approval or to give up the good fight, although it can be very hard at times.

There is no guarantee that if you do the right things, your family will experience a life of smooth sailing. Remember, we all have free will, and even God, the perfect parent, had children who rebelled when they walked with Him in the garden of Eden. We cannot expect our children and stepchildren to get through life without making mistakes or, in some cases, rebelling against God and us. However, we can rely on God to give us strength through His Holy Spirit to thrive in spite of the waves in our lives. God is our rock, our comfort, and our strength; His Word is our guide. Because of Him, we are blended, not shaken.

Questions for Discussion

1. In what ways are you showing your values to your children and stepchildren by example?

2. What is a tough situation you are facing with your blended family now?

3. Is this tough situation something you can work through, or are you ready to call it quits in this marriage?

4. Do you have a faith in God to help you through the tough times?

5. Is it worth the effort it will take to stay married to your spouse?

6. Do you feel safe in your home?

Notes

4

Look, Jerk's Mom!

One summer day as I was driving down a congested city street with my slew of sweaty kids, I stopped at a red light behind a vehicle with a personalized license plate proudly displayed on its rear bumper. One of my juvenile passengers pointed an index finger at it and exclaimed, "Look, Jerk's mom!" Sure enough, the license plate in front of us proudly proclaimed, "JKS MOM." I don't know Jerk or, more likely, Jack or Jake, but obviously his mom thinks he is pretty special. She honored him with a symbolic license plate for all to see. He may be a long-awaited child in whom the whole family rejoices. Yet her effort to honor him was misunderstood; the way she spelled it was up for interpretation. She knew what the missing letters in her message were, but the general public interpreted the message through its own filters, which were foggy at best.

The symbolism illustrated in this incident was not lost on me as I maneuvered through urban traffic with my blended brood in the backseats. When I thought about the mysterious message displayed by the mom in front of me, it struck me that in spite of our best efforts as parents, those efforts and our motives can be misunderstood by a lot of people, some of whom will jump at any opportunity to criticize us. We parents all slip up from time to time and become a type of JKS MOM. At these times a supportive family will give you the benefit of the doubt, even if they don't understand a decision you made for your children. Unintentional offenses or oversights are overlooked, and you are encouraged on your way. Apology is accepted, forgiveness is given, and everyone moves on unscathed.

On the other hand, if you are in a blended family, chances are higher that your stepchild's biological relatives will misjudge you. Be encouraged, JKS MOM! You are also pretty special to someone, your heavenly Father, and He is your guide. Stand firm in your convictions, and continue to do what is right for the children in your charge.

Unfortunately, your children's other parents may use your unintentional offenses against you. These perceived offenses could be manipulated to prove your unsuitability as a parent. They could be whispered into the ear of a child who is caught in the middle of a custody battle. When typed out like this, in black and white, it sounds absurd that any parent would use a child in order to win approval, take sole custody, or to one-up the stepparent he or she sees as a threat. It happens frequently, however, and the child is like the monkey in the middle who never wins. Consequently, that child lives in a battle zone instead of living surrounded by the mutual love and acceptance of all his or her parents in a supportive family.

An example of this kind of misunderstanding in my family involved a comment I made to Samantha. First I would like to give a little backstory. I attended middle school in an era just after Twiggy became an icon in the modeling industry. Skinny was in. A compliment of the highest order was, "Wow, you have lost weight! When you turn sideways you disappear!" I am embarrassed to confess that in my circle there were also many conversations involving the desirability of a tiny hiney, and I even heard it said that "so-and-so is really nice even though he (or she) has a bubble butt." Although I did not say this out loud, I have to admit that I agreed that skinny was better. Apparently this idea was embedded in my soul, because about twenty years later I complimented Samantha by saying, "You have no butt." Samantha's culture of origin was quite different from that of Scottsdale in 1974, and when she told her grandmother what I had said, it was as if I had punched Samantha in the face, only worse. I had offended her and her family. Samantha told me of their displeasure in response to my comment. When I let my imagination fly, I can imagine that her family might have thought I had given her a lifelong body image conflict and that I could be thought of as an unsuitable caregiver because I had cut her down. I still hang my head in misery when I think of that incident. From that experience I learned to be much more careful about what I said to her and tried to look at things from her family's perspective. I am sure I never achieved 100 percent in this area. Fortunately, they have been kind to me in spite of my putting my foot in my mouth. By the way, her family never mentioned it to me, and Samantha has a healthy self-image and holds no grudge about that incident, although it has come up at lunch with my daughters when they launched a "Remember when ..." conversation.

I want to encourage you to do the right thing every day, even if you are misunderstood. As you live an exemplary life in front of your stepchildren, they will likely come to the realization that you are worthy of their respect, eventually. In fact, your stepchildren may be confused by nasty comments made about you by their other family, because they love and respect you. On the other hand, it may take a long time to gain their respect. Either way, your loving consistency is a building block to a close relationship with them.

The Bible says in 2 Chronicles 20:17, "You need not fight in this battle; station yourselves, stand and see the salvation of the Lord on your behalf, O Judah and Jerusalem. Do not fear or be dismayed; tomorrow go out and face them, for the Lord is with you."

I am comforted to know the Lord is with me. Whether you have many people opposing you about the way you are raising your stepchildren or not, you have a God who sees it all and is going before you in everything.

Another Scripture that comforts me is Psalm 55:22: "Cast your cares on the LORD and he will sustain you; he will never let the righteous be shaken" (NIV).

If you are in Christ, you have nothing to fear, for He will never let you fall.

Questions for Discussion

1. Think about a time when you were misjudged in your role as a stepparent. How did you feel?

2. How did you respond?

3. Is there truth to what was said about you?

4. Is there anything you need to do about it?

5. Have you been able to forgive?

6. Have you made hasty judgments about the children's other family?

7. Have you improved in your understanding of the other family members' points of view—including the ex-spouse, ex-spouse-in-law, the children's other stepparents, or the children's other grandparents?

8. Have they attempted to understand you?

9. Have you attempted to understand why they oppose you (if they do)?

10. In what ways have you become a stronger person because of opposition in your life?

11. In what ways have you shown grace to others?

Notes

Grace That's Yours

A young wife and mother of several children told me this story: She and her family had come from a church that embraced them, and she had received salvation in that church. Her life had been restored; she had been forgiven and pardoned of all sin by the God of the universe. When her family was transferred because of her husband's job, they struggled to find a church family like the one they had left behind. They eventually found a church and became involved.

One day one of her children told a congregant that she was going to visit her dad. The mother told me, "Once they knew that these children were not all my husband's, we were shunned. It really hurt, because some of the people there were also friends of his from work." The self-righteous response of the congregation was devastating. The family felt alienated and judged by the congregation and stopped going to church.

Let me get this straight. These folks in the congregation were following God, who had forgiven this woman of all of her sins, but they could not forgive her? Is acceptance into the church now viewed like a life insurance application where if you answer yes to any question in section one, you are declined access to the fold? Were these other congregants without sin? Of course not.

Once you have accepted Christ, your sins—anything you have done or will do, even your thoughts that are off of the mark—are forgiven. Whether your sin is that you turn to a box of chocolate instead of to the Lord to alleviate stress or that you are divorced or selfish or any other unrighteous thing, you are forgiven—past, present, and future. Our sinfulness is more than our behavior; it is our nature. Therefore, if we behave well, there is still sin to be dealt with. Fortunately for us, God has provided the way to have our sin eradicated.

John 3:16 states, "For God so loved the world, that He gave His one and only Son, that whoever believes in him shall not perish, but have eternal life" (NIV). Period. It only takes belief in Christ as our Savior to be forgiven of all sin.

Hebrews 8:12 says, "For I will forgive their wickedness, and will remember their sins no more" (NIV).

We live in assurance that God has forgiven us of our divorces, even if they were our fault and not the fault of our ex-spouses at all. We are given a new start and can live our lives, not without consequences for the divorce, but in complete forgiveness. This is good news. Please internalize it. When you come up against criticism or hard times, if you are shunned because of your past, realize that from God's perspective you are blameless because of the sacrifice of Christ. You are precious in His sight.

Consider 1 John 1:9, which says, "If we confess our sins, He is faithful and just and will forgive us our sins and purify us from all unrighteousness" (NIV).

This is a promise to us as Christians and includes all sin, including the sin of adultery. Jesus dealt with a woman caught in the act of adultery. The story begins in John 8:3–5, which says, "The teachers of the law and the Pharisees brought in a woman caught in adultery. They made her stand before the group and said to Jesus, 'Teacher, this woman was caught in the act of adultery, In the Law Moses commanded us to stone such a woman. Now what do you say?'" (NIV).

When Jesus said, "Let any one of you who is without sin be the first to throw a stone at her," her accusers realized their own sin and left (John 8:7 NIV). Then Jesus told the woman, "Neither do I condemn you … Go now and leave your life of sin" (John 8:11 NIV).

Jesus did not condone her sin, but He forgave her sin. He told her to sin no more, to repent. Jesus put no further conditions on her freedom.

Jesus sets us free. Completely. He loves us. Completely. We are forgiven. Completely.

How does that make you feel? It makes me feel elated. It makes me want to do better from now on. I know I will fail at things and make the wrong choices from time to time. However, I want to do better, not because I will gain more favor with God. That would be impossible; He already loves me completely. I want to do better because I now understand the love of God. Paul's words in Philippians 3:13–14 further describe my thoughts: "Brethren, I do not regard myself as having laid hold of it yet; but one thing I do: forgetting what lies behind and reaching forward to what lies ahead, I press on toward the goal for the prize of the upward call of God in Christ Jesus" (NASB).

This Scripture has volumes written about it for study and debate, but for today, let's just acknowledge that even Paul, who wrote a good chunk of the New Testament, realized that he had not arrived at perfection. Neither have we. However, we can press on, doing what is right to the best of our ability. We know that we are living with full pardon for all our sin. Paul discusses "forgetting" what is past. We should still take stock and learn from the past, but we should not live in regret of the past. We are free.

Think of Genesis 19:26, when Lot's wife looked back upon Sodom and became a pillar of salt. God had given clear instructions to Lot and his family not to look back when leaving Sodom. God made a means of escape for them. Looking back, with her heart still in Sodom, meant her ruin. Do not look back longingly on the lifestyle that brought about ruin for you. Press on and see the deliverance of God.

Assuming that you are in a safe marriage without abuse, dangerous addiction, or infidelity, staying married this time, for the sake of God, for the sake of the children, and for your own sake, in spite of the difficulties, offers countless rewards.

Questions for Discussion

1. Have you experienced criticism for divorcing?

2. Is any of the criticism legitimate?

3. If so, have you repented?

4. Has God forgiven you for all your sin?

5. How do you feel about that?

6. What do you want to do in regard to your marriage because of God's love for you?

7. Do you long for the past? If so, what about it do you long for? Would it benefit you and your family to pursue those things?

8. What steps do you and your spouse take to preserve and improve your marriage?

9. What benefits have you experienced as a result of your commitment to your marriage?

10. What benefits have your children and stepchildren experienced as a result of your committed marriage?

Notes

The Basics of the Blended Family

Blended families are born from brokenness. Even if you are currently married to Mr. or Mrs. Wonderful, your children's parents are no longer a couple. Perhaps either you or your spouse had children out of wedlock and you have never been married. Perhaps you or your spouse has been widowed or divorced. There are a multitude of types of blended families, but all were formed because of some sort of prior relationship ending.

I never wanted to be divorced. It was not my dream to be a bride and then a divorcée. There came a point in my marriage when I knew there was no other reasonable option but to separate from my husband. I was still open to a miracle restoration of our marriage, but I knew I had to immediately get my children and myself out of a very bad environment. It was a devastating realization that my dreams were dashed and it was time to move on.

After moving on, I found I had new problems to work out. If you are in a blended family because of divorce and remarriage, you must have had irreconcilable differences with your ex-spouse. This was true for me. Once divorced, those differences don't go away. In fact, they will most likely intensify as you co-parent from different homes.

Your ex-spouse will probably not go away either. You may have to face the reality that your children's parent could be involved in a considerable amount of your life, at least until the children are grown and out on their own. Even after the children are grown, there are many family events where you will probably have some contact with your ex-spouse: weddings, funerals, holidays, birthdays, and events involving grandchildren, to name a few.

If you are not divorced but are contemplating it, I hope you will consider the difficulty of being divorced from all angles before you take that step. There may be legitimate complaints in your current situation, but divorce brings a whole new set of problems and challenges. Financial difficulties generally increase. Children tend to struggle academically at least for a while after a family splits. Your time may be more consumed with day-to-day shuttling of children because you are the only one available to drive them. Yard work and house work doubles if these were responsibilities you and your spouse shared. Who takes care of the cars and hot water heater, and who pays the bills? You will need extra time with your children to talk, contemplate life, and help them work through the pain of losing time with their other parent or with you.

All children, no matter how shielded they may be, are influenced by outside sources. Peers, culture, and media influence the children in both intact families and broken homes. In a blended family, the complexity of this influence can be much more confusing because of the additional input from each of biological parent. Each parent's lifestyle may be very different. In some cases, the other parent's input is contradictory to your values. How do children, to whom both parents are authorities, sort out the different rules, schedules, morals, and priorities at each of their homes? This is an enormous undertaking for children who may not be at an age to even sort their own socks. They need parents who are willing to work things out for them, to come along side them, and to show them how to cope. If both parents can work together on this, everyday life will be easier for the children.

Sometimes, try as you might, you and your ex cannot agree on rules for the children. Hard as it is, you have to let go of the idea that you can control the children's other household. You have no other option than to allow the children to follow their other parent's rules at their other parent's house. They may have chores at one home and not at another. If this is the case, the parent who implements chores at home will probably meet with resistance from the children.

Another common area of disagreement for parents in separate homes involves watching television and movies. If you forbid R-rated movies and the child's other parent doesn't, what do you do when the child watches an R-rated movie with the other parent's permission at the other parent's house? The child shouldn't be punished for watching a movie that the other parent let him or her watch, even if you won't allow it at your house.

As long as the child is not in danger of physical harm or deprivation of food or medical attention, the courts will not do anything to enforce your rules. It is not illegal to let children do things that you may consider to be immoral or harmful to their psyches. Your list of grievances may be quite long and include differences in bedtimes, cleanliness, clothing styles, television shows, diet, dating, driving, and money. Keep in mind that the nature of the broken home lends itself to these differences; you probably do not have the power to make decisions that will govern all aspects of your children's lives when they are away with their other parent.

Most parents have rules for behavior, and conflicts over those rules can get sticky. Things can get really messy, however, when you are on a different spiritual plane than the parents in the other home. You do have the ability to teach your beliefs to your children even if those beliefs go against their other family's beliefs. The children in this situation will take time to sort out what you say and weigh it with what they are being taught in their other home. Eventually they will make their own decisions.

Think about how you would treat a conversation about something your children learned at school or on the street with which you disagree. If it is important, you want to talk about it with the children. The same is true of things your children are taught by their other parent. If you disagree with the teaching, consider with care how you will convey your thoughts without being cruel or rude about their other parent. Try to separate yourself from the emotions you may feel about the conflicting teaching. Then teach your values and beliefs regardless of the opposing information they are getting in their other home. You may experience some backlash from the other parent, but you can't let the children grow up oblivious to your values.

For example, let's say that you are trying to teach your teen to guard his or her heart. What does that mean? This is not something that is the cultural norm, but let's imagine that to you it is important.

Proverbs 4:23 gives the instruction and the reason: "Watch over your heart with all diligence, for from it flow the springs of life" (NASB).

Discuss how to make this a practical application in life. Be specific. For example, you could say to your teen, "Decide ahead of time that you will not have sex before marriage."

Your teen may respond, "Why?"

"Because when you give your heart to someone through sex, you are not taking care of it as you were instructed. This will affect the springs of life."

"What?"

"In other words, your spiritual vitality."

"What?"

"The way you respond to everything and the way you live your life; wounded or not, strong or weak in spirit, impulsive or purposeful. It is really important to me to know that you understand that this is what I believe to be best for you. I know that in our culture there are many people not adhering to this value, but there are a lot of problems that come along with having sex outside of the marriage covenant. I would like you to understand this, so let's talk more about it, okay?"

I think most people will agree that it is important to prepare ahead of time in this way for situations that may arise in order to lessen the chances of being taken off-guard. You can see that this will take a lot of talking, and the other household may have adults in positions of authority who contradict you. In the example conversation there was nothing directly said about what the other parent may believe or the way the other parent might be living, but the truth was stated and the conversation begun.

In a blended family you may have the children's other parents working against your efforts in addition to the common teen communication barrier, even if you are raising a *compliant teen*, a term that may be an oxymoron. As it is the nature of teens to test, stretch themselves, and break away from their parents as they become adults, you may not know any compliant teens. This makes communication and the implementation of rules harder in a blended family than in an intact family. Consider the weight of the issue being taught in opposition to what you teach your children. If the children are allowed to eat cupcakes in bed at Dad's and not at your house, you can let it slide. If it is about something non-negotiable, you need to speak up. Talk to these young people in your care with warmth and understanding along with steadfastness when it comes to your non-negotiable principles. You cannot ignore your children's development. To be silent is not nice. Sometimes we have to make waves as parents, but it is better to make waves now than to live with dire consequences later.

Constructive communication with a stepchild, especially an older child or teen, can be much more difficult to accomplish than with your biological child. The relationship that allows you to have an actual conversation with this person, who is accustomed to abbreviated text messages, is best built through the years when he or she is young, flexible, and basically your captive audience.

Herein lies the most challenging aspect of stepparenting. If your stepparent relationship begins later in the lives of the stepchildren, keep in mind that your stepkids do not likely know you or even trust you. Unity with these children's biological parent, to whom you are married, must be developed. Then, in unity, the parent and stepparent can together guide the teen. The teen may accept the guidance of the biological parent with whom he or she has a relationship and file away his or her observation of the stepparent's unity with his or her biological parent for a later time.

When I say *later*, I mean it could be years before your steadfast unity and diligence mean anything at all to this child. Your children simply may not buy into your whole new family configuration. Remember, they had a family before, and they were probably pretty content with it before it was ripped apart. Things changed, and they might not like the way it worked out. You can't rush the process. The child controls the timeline of the relationship's growth.

I recently had a conversation with a woman who is engaged to be married. Her five-year-old daughter loves the man who will become her stepfather. When the woman and her fiancé told the children about their plan to marry, they all continued to enjoy the evening together. As her fiancé was leaving he told the child, "I love you." Her reply was, "I love you, too, but please don't marry my mom."

I understand where she is coming from. When my oldest child, Cameron, was a baby his great-grandmother told me, "Children are creatures of habit. They love routine." The children in a remarriage situation have had their lives turned upside down by their parent moving away or passing away. It is understandable that they might not want a new stepparent to disrupt their lives again. This can be felt as a threat to their security, even if they love the person who is marrying into their family.

Complexities abound before, during, and after a divorce, but in this situation my observation is that the hardest thing for the children to come to terms with is the new stepparent. As wonderful as your new spouse may be, the kids already have, or had, a parent who was like God to them. This intruder cannot replace that parent, ever.

Even if you, as a couple, are united in every important way, the kids can still end up being at odds with everyone, including each other and all their parental figures.

Let's take a look at it from the children's perspective. If you have four bosses at work, all at the same level of management, all telling you what to do, all saying different things, and all saying that the other bosses are inept, to whom would you listen, and how long would you stay at that job?

Likewise, the child in a blended family has the biological parent and stepparent, maybe another biological parent, and maybe another stepparent, all in authority over him or her. The child may not have an established relationship with either stepparent. The no-brainer here is for the child to dismiss both stepparents' authority, thereby simplifying his or her life.

Then let's imagine that the child has two contemptuous biological parents giving contradictory instructions, living very different moral lives from each other. It makes me want to cover my ears and scream just to think about putting myself in that child's shoes. Do you wonder why a stepparent might have a hard time getting through to this child? The child's ears are covered, and it would take a generous portion of grace and adept maneuvering to pry those little hands away from his or her ears. No matter how great a stepparent you are, there is much less chance the child will let any of your input penetrate his or her spirit.

In addition to the disruption of the child's "perfect" previous family, the birth order has been rearranged. Maybe your son was the oldest child in the family, and now he has older stepsiblings. The baby of the family may have the perspective that she has lost her position to younger, more time-intensive or more "adorable" children. Maybe the child is an only child in one home and part of a group in another. You might have multiple children who are very close in age, making the household seem more like a classroom or youth group than a family. This is not impossible to overcome, but it can be difficult.

You, stepparents, have a challenge on your hands. That is the nature of the blended family, because it was born out of brokenness. It is easier to conquer the challenges when you break them down into manageable pieces. Determine what you can control. Here are four things that you can control.

Thing one: You can love your spouse and show love to the children.

Thing two: You can control what you say.

Thing three: You can enforce the rules of your house.

Thing four: You can rely on God and pray for your family.

I know firsthand the challenges you face. As a stepparent I had to realize that some things were simply out of my control. I hope to encourage you throughout this book by helping you take note of the things you can control and helping you take a humorous look at blended family life.

Questions for Discussion

1. How can you relate to what you have just read?

2. Do some of these issues sound familiar?

3. What do you do in a situation in which the other parent has very different ideas about what the children should be allowed to do?

4. Considering this chapter's subject, what are some related issues you are dealing with currently?

5. Are there related issues you have already resolved?

6. How do you feel about letting go of control when your children are at their other parent's home?

7. How do you think you can best help your children to sort out the differences in your rules, schedules, morals, and priorities?

8. Are you and your children's other biological parent willing to work on these things to benefit your children?

9. How would you describe your children's relationship with their stepparent(s)?

Notes

Exactly How Are We Related?

The topic of this chapter is one that needs to be addressed, but it comes with a warning. It may be hard to follow. The blended family structure is hard to discuss without losing some readers in the complexity along the way. For that, I apologize. Please stick with my story here, and I think you will gain insight. I hope to show you that what you are experiencing in your family is typical of blended families.

When Stefan was about three years old, he said to me, "I know who Dad's dad is. Bob." That was true. His grandfather's name was Bob, but Bob was also the name of his stepsiblings' biological father. One Bob was Steve's dad, and the other Bob was Cameron and Whitney's dad. None of us had ever met the Bob who was Steve's dad, but Stefan thought the two Bobs were one and the same. To little Stefan, his half-brother Cameron, a teenager, was about as big as his dad, Steve; it made sense to him that these two "grown" men had the same Bob as a dad. Confusing.

Our oldest son, Cameron, now has a daughter, Roxi, who was born when Eric, our youngest, was fairly little. Shortly after Roxi's birth Cameron brought her to our house to meet the family. Eric was confused about what his becoming an uncle meant within the family's dynamics. He wondered if Uncle Jim would now be his brother, since they were now both uncles. Eric has half-siblings who have different parents from his; therefore, having the same parents was not, in his mind, a requirement for being a brother.

Eric also thought that Great-Grandma Warren would now be his dad's great-great-grandma, because I told him that Roxi made her a great-great-grandma. I didn't bother to get into the fact that Grandma Warren was a step-great-grandma to Cameron. That would have only confused Eric further.

That night while driving to church I asked our younger two boys if they felt more like uncles now that they had met their niece, Roxi. Then I added, "I don't feel too much like a grandmother, but there she is, so I am." Eric said, "You *don't* seem like a grandmother. You still drive perfectly!"

Confusion can present itself in the intact family, but throw in the complexities of a blended family and the dynamics get even more confusing to the children.

One November as I drove the carpool to school, several of the children in the car were talking about their Thanksgiving plans. One of the children asked Stefan what he does for Thanksgiving. He replied, "Samantha goes to her other mom's house. Cameron and Whitney go to Bob's house. Then Eric, Mom, Dad, and I go to Flagstaff." He sat in silence the rest of the way to school. As we pulled into the parking lot he asked, "Exactly how are we related to Bob?" He had no idea what the relationship was between Cameron and Whitney's dad and his family.

Until that day, I thought he knew. After the carpool kids had poured out of my car into the school, Stefan and I had a minute to talk in private. I explained to him in simple terms, as if for the first time: "You know I was married before, right? Well, when I was married before ..." He followed the logic and filled in the blanks in his concept of our family dynamics, and off he went to school. He had just always accepted things as they were, without question.

I sat in my car in the child drop-off lane in front of the elementary school puzzled by his unawareness. The previous family was a large part of my life, and he was a smart child, but he had never thought about those relationships to that extent until then.

Sometimes I didn't know my children had a misconception. I tried to preempt confusion by giving the children family background information on a regular basis, but as you can see, sometimes things slipped through the cracks—big things.

Our family tree was, and still is, messy. As a child I was raised in as neat a tree as you could imagine—every branch intact, children raised by their biological parents, grandparents living together until death. None of my siblings, aunts, uncles, or cousins had been divorced. Only me. I was the only divorced member of my extended family.

For a number of years I had an online business creating illustrated family tree artwork. The family tree drawings depicted a tree with a character to represent each family member sitting on the branches. Most families ordered a tree with three to four generations represented by the personalized characters. Creating these trees for people, I found that many, if not most, families' trees are not so tidy.

When I created our family tree on paper, Whitney asked, "Where are my dad and Samantha's mom going to be?" That was a common dilemma for families who ordered family tree pictures from me.

Some families who ordered these illustrated family trees put the ex-spouses on the branch with the children but apart from the divorced spouse. Some families left the ex-spouses off the tree completely and just illustrated the existing marriages. It really depended upon the recipient of the illustration and the relationships between the person and the divorced family members. When I think of this now, those illustrated family trees show me how differently each family views its relationships.

I personally find family lineage fascinating and like to have a clear understanding of who is related to whom and how. My grandmother taught me at an early age the difference between second cousins and first-cousins-once-removed.

In contrast, there are those who call every close friend Aunt or Uncle and don't seem to keep track at all. Some require children to call a stepdad Dad, and others use first names. Some families call a live-in girlfriend Stepmom. Remember the movie by that name? In the 1998 movie, Isabel, played by Julia Roberts, was not even married to Luke, who was played by Ed Harris. Therefore, she was not technically a stepmom but a live-in girlfriend. That movie title has always bothered me, but when I mention it to most people, even likeminded Christians, they haven't given it a second thought. In my mind, Mom is a title to be revered and adored, not bestowed on the current girlfriend who also happens to babysit your kids. My own stepdaughter has never called me Mom, and I helped raise her from the age of six. She refers to me as her stepmom or bonus mom, but she calls me Ginny.

Some children don't care in the least about their family tree. However, your children and stepchildren may find comfort in knowing how the branches of their family tree fit together. Children generally like order. Be prepared to explain the dynamics of the family tree to them as they become old enough to understand and when they want to know.

It can be a shock for your children when they finally put together that their stepbrother's grandma is not really their grandma or that you used to be married to someone else or had children out of wedlock. As children are ready to understand, you may also find yourself having conversations about the bad choices made in your past and why those choices were not best.

I don't want my children to think that because I was divorced and remarried and lived to tell the tale that marriage vows are to be taken lightly or that my path is okay. I point out how the choices I made continue to impact our family at children's ballgames, weddings, graduations, and holidays, as well as in everyday life.

Unless they are completely estranged or have passed away, chances are good that your former family members are somehow involved in your life and the lives of your children and, to take it further, the lives of your grandchildren.

I had a conversation with my granddaughter Roxi when she was eight years old about her visit with my ex-in-laws, who are her great-grandparents. Also in attendance at the visit were my ex-sister-in-law, Alyson, and her children, who are Roxi's cousins (first-cousins-once-removed). In the lighthearted conversation it was easy to share her excitement about the visit. I even pointed out the relationship that Alyson's children have with my brother's children through their basketball team. Roxi was delighted to put it all together. These cousins are friends with those cousins!

I have talked to people who have a very difficult time with those ex-family gatherings. It is not unusual to feel anger toward an ex-spouse or his or her family. The anger could be justified. However, as the adult in the situation, your behavior toward the ex-family members must be civil. What your children see will impact them one way or the other. If you let the children see your resentment, it only makes it harder on them.

The dynamics of the blended family are really confusing, and I find it a little mind boggling to write about it in an orderly fashion. I hope that in reading about my family you will see that you are not alone in this messiness. Blended families are complex by nature. If you present the relationships to your children in a matter-of-fact and kind manner, they will be less likely to harbor resentment and more likely to accept things as they are.

Questions for Discussion

1. Have your children asked about the relationships in your family?

2. What have you said to them about those relationships?

3. Are you at peace with your family tree, broken branches and all?

4. Does it cause you stress to talk about your children's lineage or your past?

5. How does your perspective impact your children's view of ex-family members? Are you being fair to the children in your portrayal of their other parent or grandparents?

6. Does your children's other biological parent still participate in your life?

7. Is your ex considered part of your family?

8. Is your current spouse's ex-spouse involved in your life and the lives of your children?

9. Is your ex-spouse's new spouse helping to raise your children?

10. Do you work well with these people?

11. Do you like them?

12. What have you done to build healthy, civil relationships with these people for the good of the children?

13. What could you do better?

Notes

Section 3

What Do We Do Now As We Move Forward?

8

Family Identity

In light of the previous chapter on the messiness of the blended family tree, it is important to note that there are things you can do to neaten up the messiness a bit. You have a group of children who are thrust into a family together. Some get along and some don't. Some have accepted one another as brothers and sisters and some haven't. You can't force the issue, but you can start to create your own family identity.

A mother with two young children was engaged to marry a man with two children of similar ages. She said to her son, who had been arguing with the man's children, "You should try to get along with them; they will soon be your brother and sister."

The five-year-old boy said, "I guess I am just not used to them yet."

"Well," said the mother, "remember it took you a while to get used to your own sister as well," to which the boy replied, "I'm still not really used to her yet either."

Again, the running theme is that it all takes time. To blend smoothly takes time and patience, but you can start right away to intentionally develop your family identity.

Family traditions, quotes, and tall tales are valuable tools that can be used to create a unique family identity. It gives us a sense of where we came from, our values, our sense of humor, our history, and our sense of belonging to something comfortable, unique, and bigger than ourselves. Our family's faith and foundation are transferred to us by other, usually older, family members, and these things are important to us as we each carve out our place in the big world. Having a family identity is just as important in a blended family as it is for intact families.

However, now more than ever we are shuttling our kids from one activity to another, breathlessly driving under the golden arches, handing out bags of fast food for dinner, and sending them off to bed with no more than, "Brush your teeth," in the way of conversation. We drive here and there, listening to the radio while our kids are plugged into video games, iPods pump tunes into their heads, and they text their friends; siblings sit side by side, isolated from one another. These distractions make it difficult to carve out time to share, but the value is immeasurable. Be purposeful in creating your family identity. Following are suggestions for how to build this family identity.

Take time to talk to your children, really talk to them at length, about yourself, your family growing up, and what their grandparents and great-grandparents were like. Isn't it fascinating to find out that you do something the same way that your aunt does or that you are talented in the same way that your grandfather was? Stories my maternal grandmother told me about her life gave me permission to have spontaneous fun. My paternal grandmother instilled a sense of responsibility to get a good education. All the stories my parents, grandparents, aunts, and uncles told helped shape me into who I am today and gave me a sense of my roots.

An activity that has stood the test of time when it comes to knitting families together is camping. What better time to share family history and stories than while around a campfire, enjoying s'mores and clean mountain air? We had a large, heavy canvas tent, the same tent my family camped in when I was a child. I fondly remember the smell of the damp canvas, dirt, and pine. The tent was stored in a separate storage bag from its metal tent poles because it was all so big and unwieldy. When camping, our children chopped wood with an ax. We hiked, and the kids played with nothing but the stuff they found in the woods. We had centerpieces of flowers that caused rashes, one baby sucked on elk poop, and one girl rolled in poison ivy because "the leaves were so pretty." "Bouncy Log" was a fallen tree that we visited time and again over the years. We know, because we took groups there on more than one occasion, that Bouncy Log was big enough for twenty people to stand on at one time. It stretched across a small ravine. It was fun to be on it and bounce. It became a tradition within a tradition to go to Bouncy Log when we went camping. Conversations come up and opportunities to bond are natural in a setting devoid of television, phone calls, and scheduled activities, school, and sport practices.

Family traditions are important for building the family identity and seem to come naturally with holidays and birthdays. In between special occasions, implement traditions as simple as having no electronic entertainment on Mondays in order to enjoy more productive time together. A half hour for bedtime tuck-in with stories, private talks, and prayers will nurture relationships and deepen the children's sense of belonging. Taking this time, one on one, helps each child feel valued.

Working as a team on a project, such as gardening for Grandma, volunteering together at a community food bank, or making homemade gift-wrap, can enhance your family identity and relationships.

Throughout your day express positive observations about your family to your children, such as "I'm so glad we live in a family that can talk about anything" or "I love that my children are each others' best friends." When correcting your children, say, "Our family doesn't call each other names" or "We don't spit on the playground" or "Our family likes to be polite, kind, and helpful to others."

Use your creativity to think of things that will work for your family members' interests and schedules. Make what you choose an integral part of all your lives. It will enrich your children's lives and create an important foundation for your family identity.

Start today to create a strong family identity. Offer the children a deeper understanding of who they are and where they fit into your family and the world. You may be surprised at the way working and planning together builds lasting bonds in your blended family.

Questions for Discussion

1. What are some characteristics that define your family?

2. What traditions have you carried from your past that you still implement today?

3. What are some new traditions that have started with your new family?

4. Are these important to your children?

5. Are there some traditions your children or stepchildren would like to add to your blended family?

6. What are some projects you could work on as a family?

7. What are some things you already do to establish yourselves as a family?

8. Have you experienced resistance from the children or your spouse in your efforts to build a family identity?

9. What is your favorite idea for developing a family identity?

10. How can you start implementing that one thing right now?

Notes

Things You Can Control: Thing One

Love Your Spouse and Show Love to the Children

According to Charles Shedd, "A father's first responsibility to his child is to love his wife. The most favored children in the world are those whose parents love each other." Shedd may not have been speaking of stepparents when he made this proclamation, but failure is often the outcome when the family structure is out of whack. As the Bible says, "If a house is divided against itself, that house will not be able to stand" (Mark 3:25 NASB). The design of the family is to have the parents united in the lead, loving each other and together loving the children as welcome additions to their family.

One of our children, at an early age, said about Steve and me, "You talk about everything." It does take a lot of talking to dwell in unity with your spouse. To agree on everything is highly unlikely, but as far as the children are concerned, if you show a chink in your unity, they will pry it apart as fast as they can. This is why it is better to discuss your differences in parental decisions apart from the children and always approach them as a united team.

If it is possible, try to have unity with the children's absent biological parent as well. Children are more secure with parents who are united and who treat one another in a loving manner.

There are many Scriptures on loving your spouse, and they are logical. Ephesians 5:33 says, "However, each one of you also must love his wife as he loves himself, and the wife must respect her husband" (NIV). Ephesians 5:25 states, "Husbands, love your wives, just as Christ loved the church and gave Himself up for her" (NIV).

In an intact family, the parents' relationship exists before there are children. The family unit is formed at the altar between husband and wife, who love each other. The children come along as welcome additions to the family; therefore, it is natural for the parents to hold the marriage relationship in the highest regard.

In a blended family, at least some of the children existed before the marriage and, in most cases, before the relationship between the husband and wife. Therefore, even though the husband and wife love each other, there are other people in the home expecting their undivided attention.

The wife does things with her kids her way, and the husband does things with his kids his way. While this may also be the case in an intact family, those parents have the luxury of getting to discuss how they will raise their kids prior to having children, which enables them to develop common goals and strategies.

The children of a blended family are already living by the rules and customs of at least one parent whose rules and customs may be different from that of the stepparent. Confusion sets in, tensions rise, and children will react or respond in a variety of negative ways. I believe it was Josh McDowell who originally coined the statement, "Rules without relationship leads to rebellion." It has become such a popular buzz line that it is hard to say where I first heard it, but I have found it to be especially true for stepparents dealing with stepchildren. When the response of the children is not positive, discipline or direction is necessary. A relationship built on love and trust needs to be in place before a stepparent's discipline will provide effective training for the children, and that sort of relationship can take years to build. You may have just jumped into the middle of your stepchildren's lives, or you may not have many years to cultivate that type of relationship because the stepchild is a teen and will be grown and gone soon.

All through the Bible we are commanded to love one another. John 13:34 says, "A new command I give to you: Love one another. As I have loved you, so you must love one another" (NIV). The Greek word for love used here is *agapo*, meaning to love in a social or moral sense, acting in a loving manner, as opposed to *agape*, meaning affection or benevolent love. Leviticus 19:18 says, "Do not seek revenge or bear a grudge against anyone among your people, but love your neighbor as yourself. I am the LORD" (NIV). Ephesians 5:2 says, "And walk in the way of love, just as Christ loved us and gave himself up for us as a fragrant offering and sacrifice to God" (NIV).

Now consider Matthew 5:44–48, which says, "But I tell you: Love your enemies and pray for those who persecute you, that you may be sons of your Father in heaven. He causes His sun to rise on the evil and the good, and sends rain on the righteous and the unrighteous. If you love those who love you, what reward will you get? Are not even the tax collectors doing that? And if you greet only your brothers, what are you doing more than others? Do not even pagans do that? Be perfect, therefore, as your heavenly Father is perfect" (NIV). *Perfect* here means mature and complete in the likeness of God.

This kind of love is a lofty aspiration in some blended families where resentment toward stepparents may run high, but it is well worth the effort to achieve the goal of loving even the most obstinate stepchild. In Jesus' own words, this is a *command*, not a suggestion. The stepchild may not love you, and you may not feel an emotional love for the child, but there is no excuse for any family member to treat another poorly.

One avenue to take toward building a relationship with stepchildren is also a wonderful tool to use with your spouse and biological children. As I said, children will not respond well to rules placed on them without the development of the relationship first. The tool I recommend is to identify your family members' love languages. In the book *The Five Love Languages* by Gary Chapman, these love languages are discussed in detail.[9] In a nutshell, here is a short description for each love language and a suggestion for how to use it.

1. Quality time: If one of your stepchildren (or anyone else in the family) expresses love through sharing quality time, join the child in his or her interests.
2. Encouraging words: Praise and compliment the child with genuine words.
3. Physical touch and closeness: Some children like hugs or just sitting in close proximity to others.
4. Acts of service: Help the child with something, such as homework or a project, run an errand for the child, or give him or her a ride somewhere.
5. Gift giving (or receiving): If gift giving is one of your stepchildren's love language, remember that the gifts can be small—a card, flowers, a new book, Twizzlers, or anything else that he or she likes.

As you get to know your stepchildren, their love languages will become more obvious to you. Observe your family members to see how they show love. Does the child draw you a picture and give it to you tied with a ribbon, or does he or she touch people while talking to them? Does the child help his or her mom fluff pillows on the sofa, or does the child compliment others? Does he or she watch a ballgame just to be with you? The way he or she shows love to others is the way he or she will feel love coming from you.

If you are a gift giver, and the child views love as spending quality time together, you can miss out on a growing relationship because you give love in a way that does not register with the child's idea of what love is. No matter how many gifts you give him or her, the child just wants your time. Watch closely, and love your stepchildren in the ways they receive it best. Mastering the love languages can help build a bridge into your stepchildren's hearts.

Despite your best efforts, the kids may take a very long time to accept the new family. Hang in there. You will benefit from the act of loving even if the stepchild never accepts you.

A pastor told me years ago, "You are trying to form this new family, and your kids aren't buying it." It was true. My four-year-old child sat as far as she could from Steve at the dining room table and muttered to herself, "Don't worry. Pretty soon he will go back to his own house."

This sentiment is not unusual. Don't let your feelings of rejection or discouragement get in the way of continuing to love. I have been in that hard place, and I know how it feels. I also know the rewards of continuing to fight for the hearts of my children and stepchild. That stepfather, Steve, never went "back to his own house," and in time the child began to trust and love him. Now Whitney is twenty-seven, and the two of them have a growing, trusting, loving, and caring relationship, but it took years to get to that point. The turning point came when she was eighteen years old, which was fourteen years into my marriage to Steve.

Most stepparents would gladly start a mutually caring relationship right away, but it is the child who determines the timeframe and the closeness of the relationship. The children can't be rushed, but in their time, if you are a faithful stepparent, they will begin to soften. Sometimes all you can do is pray and wait.

Here is something you can do with your family. Even children who are not buying into your new family might be happy to talk about how they like to be shown love. Write down each of your family members' names. After a brief description of each of the five love languages, ask each family member to share which one is his or her love language. Before you share your love language with the others, you might even ask them to tell you what they think your love language is. Then share your love language with them along with an example of something specific that would show love to you. Make it something simple that any one of them could do.

Ask each family member to share one example of something that would make him or her feel loved. Then do those things for one another. Let the children act independently, and look for an opportunity to show love to the other family members.

The next time you have an opportunity, maybe at dinner a few days later or at a family outing, share with one another some things you noticed that communicated love.

Questions for Discussion

1. Is your relationship with your spouse the priority in your family?

2. Do you feel secure in your relationship with your spouse?

3. Do you understand why it is best when the marriage relationship is the priority?

4. How has your blended family experience differed from your expectations?

5. Do you have difficult relationships in your extended stepfamily?

6. How are you working toward improving those relationships?

7. What is beyond your control that you need to let go of?

8. How can you support your spouse in his or her role as a stepparent?

9. What do you do in order for your children to feel loved by you?

10. Do they feel loved by your spouse?

11. Do you feel loved by your family?

Notes

Things You Can Control: Thing Two

Preserve Your Life: Hold Your Tongue

You can control what you say. Imagine yourself as a child. Put yourself in that place and time, young and unaware of your parents' problems. You love your father. You hear your mother on a tirade about him as she speaks to a friend about the trials she is suffering as a result of your father's actions. Maybe what she is saying is true; maybe it is not. That doesn't matter to you. All you know is that you hear it over and over again, and then you go to your father's house and hear things just as bad about your mother. How does that make you feel? Confused, sad, angry, guilty?

These people, your parents, are like God to you. They are your protectors and providers. In your opinion, your mom is the most loving person you know, and your dad is the strongest dad in the world. You are secure in your home and know your parents love you. Then one day it all falls apart.

Perhaps your family's scenario is different than the one I have illustrated. There are as many variables as there are broken marriages. However, one consistent truth is that you will bring about ruin if you don't hold your tongue. Proverbs 13:3 says, "Those who guard their lips preserve their lives, but those who speak rashly will come to ruin" (NIV).

Sometimes it is difficult to resist speaking poorly of your ex-spouse, but giving in to the urge is very damaging to children. They do not benefit from hearing about the contemptibility of their other parent, and it enhances your own bitterness. If you allow bitterness to get a hold of you, you will be hurting yourself and your children more than you hurt your ex-spouse. As the Bible says, "Get rid of all bitterness, rage and anger, brawling and slander, along with every form of malice" (Ephesians 4:31 NIV).

It sometimes seems as though bitterness and anger have a life of their own, that they are just there and nothing can be done to make them go away. The same seems true for worry. During a particularly hard time in my life I was full of anger, worry, and dread. I tossed and turned all night long with thoughts of bad outcomes plaguing me. I had too much to deal with, and in spite of all of my prayer, these bad thoughts kept coming back, day and night.

One day I decided I would not talk or think about anything that was stressful all day; my hope was that it would help me sleep at night. I would only think good thoughts and control my mind. Philippians 4:6–9 says, "Do not be anxious about anything, but in every situation, by prayer and petition, with thanksgiving, present your requests to God. And the peace of God, which transcends all understanding, will guard your hearts and your minds in Christ Jesus. Finally, brothers and sisters, whatever is true, whatever is noble, whatever is right, whatever is pure, whatever is lovely, whatever is admirable—if anything is excellent or praiseworthy—think about such things. Whatever you have learned or received or heard from me, or seen in me—put it into practice. And the God of peace will be with you" (NIV). That very night I had the first rock solid night of sleep in weeks. Peace was with me.

It will undoubtedly take time for you to heal emotionally if your ex-spouse has treated you with disloyalty, cruelty, verbal assaults, physical abuse, or any number of other injustices. It will take time to grieve the loss of your first family, first love, and the dreams you had.

That is something you need to work through. As you go through the healing process, be diligent to hold your tongue and keep yourself from causing further damage to your children. Pray that God will put a guard at your mouth so that you will not speak of anything that will cause your children's pain to multiply.

In the context of the blended family, holding your tongue as stated in God's Word is still the truth. Consider what you think about your new spouse's ex-spouse and that extended family. Ron Deal, a professional counselor, would call your husband's ex-wife your "ex-wife-in-law." Apply the same principles of holding your tongue and not speaking poorly about the children's other family, even if the adults in that household are living immoral or destructive lives. You may be the only Christian in your stepchildren's lives. Do you want them to view Christians as bitter, jealous, resentful, or full of spite and malice toward their parents in their other home, or would you rather show them the love of God and grace for living in difficult circumstances while relying on the strength of the Lord?

Consider the little comments made under your breath, such as "We could afford that if I received child support." Or perhaps you mutter the reverse: "I would be able to afford to take you if I didn't give all my money to your mother." Or, perhaps you find yourself saying something judgmental, such as "He wouldn't be late picking you up in the morning if he wasn't out partying so late at night." These comments are like poison darts to the child's heart. A child cares about both parents and may feel a sense of responsibility over the whole situation. That is not their burden to bear. It is yours as parents.

I am not saying that you need to lie to your children to protect them from the truth. Just don't speak in a degrading or hateful manner, and don't say too much too soon. Some of what is going on will be evident to them as time goes on.

Some things definitely need to be discussed with the children for their own protection. Speak with your children as the need arises. You must talk to them about safety issues, such as drunk driving or any type of abuse. If these things are going on, steps need to be taken to protect the children, possibly through the court system. Be sure to offer to pray about the situation with the children. Praying for your ex-spouse with your children will go a long way toward the children's healing and maturing.

Dealing with the problems faced by any blended family is not ideal, but a blended family can be a wonderful, loving, and enriching environment in which to live. With your blended family, you have been given a second chance for a happy home.

After our first year of "blending" my sister said to me, "It is like you have a whole new life." My joyful response was, "I do!" The blended family I have been given is the gift of a whole new life from God, and I aim to protect and preserve it any way I can.

Remember Proverbs 13:3, which says, "Those who guard their lips preserve their lives, but those who speak rashly will come to ruin" (NIV). If you are not actively preserving your life, there is an enemy, Satan, who is out to destroy it, and he will do so wherever he can. Be cautious with your words; in them is the power to bring life or death to those you love.

Questions for Discussion

1. Have you ever said anything negative about your child's absent parent either to the child or within earshot of the child?

2. How did the child respond? Was the response a healthy response?

3. Can you think of positive things to say about your ex-spouse to your children?

4. What do you think is the benefit of building up, with truthful statements, your children's absent parent when talking about him or her to your children?

5. Is there anything harmful happening to the children in their other parent's home?

6. What can you do differently this week to be an encouragement with regard to your children's absent parent?

7. Do you tell your children that you love, care about, or hope for the best for their other parent?

Notes

Things You Can Control: Thing Three

Enforce the Rules of Your House

I touched on this subject earlier and want to delve more deeply into the subject now. Rules may vary from your home to your children's or stepchildren's other home. That is okay. The children may threaten, argue, or beg, but you are the boss in your home. It can be disheartening or even scary to stand firm when the children say, "Fine, I'll just go to Dad's!" or "Mom always lets me …" The truth is that once the children reach a certain age, they may make the choice to live where the rules are more lax. Unity between all the adults would be preferable, but such unity is not likely, considering that there may be four or more parents in charge of each child.

Assess your rules; are they based in morality, or are they morally neutral? Can you live with an unmade bed in the child's room? Do you let your children date at fourteen years of age? You need to decide which hill to die on. Once you and your spouse are sure, as a united authority, of the rules to which you want to adhere, be consistent. If the children have reached an age when reason can be used (which may not happen until they are grown and gone), go ahead and reason with them. Whether the other home has the stricter rules or it is the other way around, the things I am about to say still apply.

Once you have decided what they are, stick to the rules for your family no matter what the kids are allowed to do in their other home. There is no way you can impose your rules in the other home of your children or stepchildren. Furthermore, although the rules may be different in different homes, it would be wrong to have different rules for different children in your own home. This sounds so obvious in writing, but it can be a hurdle in real life. Remember, in your home you are a whole family unit with your own identity. You can tell your kids, all of them, to obey your rules while they are in your care.

You cannot, however, impose your rules on them while they are with the other parent. You can appeal to the other parent to enforce a rule and explain your position, but he or she may not agree with your stance and refuse to hold to it. If that is the case, you should not punish the child for doing what the other parent permits when the child is under the other parent's care.

For example, you may have fairly strict guidelines as to the content of the movies that you allow your children to see. Their other families may not hold the same standard. This is an opportunity to empower the children to make good choices at their other parent's home. When at the other parent's house, the children are not likely forced to watch an R-rated movie or to have their boyfriends in their bedrooms, for example. Even if rules are lax over there, they can choose to adhere to the standards set in your home. Make your morals, values, ethics, and the source of those clear to your children when they are mature enough to understand.

I recall hearing about a family situation in which a father simply told his young daughter why he thought it was not best for her to watch R-rated movies when she was with her mother's family. He said to her, "You don't have to watch those movies just because they are on. You can find something to do in another room." This empowered the child to make the decision for herself to watch or not to watch. There was no condemnation from her father if she did watch, but he was not backing down from his standard. The rule in his house was not changed.

While a child from an intact family probably will not have to exercise this initiative at such an early age, it is something valuable to teach all children. The ability to make choices that oppose the popular choice is a tool that the child can use in any situation, whether with friends, schoolmates, or family. At times when the consequences of the wrong choice may be direr, this tool is particularly valuable. It is good practice for life.

Questions for Discussion

1. Are you and your spouse in agreement on most house rules?

2. Is there a moral difference in the rules of your home and the children's other home(s), or are they morally neutral?

3. Is the children's safety at stake or is anything illegal involving or exposed to the children in the other home(s)?

4. How will you reconcile the differences between your home and the other home(s)?

5. What rules can you let go of, if any?

6. How can you empower your children to make good choices when they are away from your home?

Notes

Things You Can Control: Thing Four

Rely on God and Pray

Let's say that you newlyweds, in perfect unity, have one child who opposes at least one of you. Add to that your ex-spouses, who also oppose you. You, my friends, are outnumbered from the start. What can you do in a case like that? Honestly, the odds are against you, but you have a God who is bigger than all of it. How, in real life, do you tap into His strength in order to benefit the children and stay in charge of your children and in love with your family?

First of all, realize that your struggle is primarily a spiritual battle. You have to be prepared. We have an enemy who is out to steal, kill, and destroy. Destruction of the family is devastating on so many levels: to the parents, children, aunts, uncles, grandparents, and eventually the children's children; and the cycle continues. It affects friends, work, and productivity in the classroom. The ripple effect is astounding. Doesn't it make sense that the Enemy would want to destroy families? For him it is a win-win situation to destroy the family in this generation and, as a result, the next generation and more.

As a mother and stepmother, I often felt as if I had to do something to right a situation. It wasn't always natural to pray first, but as time went on I came to realize that prayer was not just my first defense but also my first *offense*. Prayer is an action. Prayer is powerful against the Enemy. It can calm us and help us think and respond more clearly to challenges we face. Praying reveals the hand of God in ways you may not expect. I have seen for myself and heard from others many accounts of God going before His people into custody or child support court. I have seen God move "mountains" in rebellious children's hearts. We have spiritual authority over our children. Because we have an enemy, we need to be communicating with the one who has already defeated him. As the Bible says, "Be alert and of sober mind. Your enemy the devil prowls around like a roaring lion looking for someone to devour" (1 Peter 5:8 NIV).

The Enemy is after your kids! Don't give that light consideration. It is common for us to forget to pray when things are running smoothly or even in the heat of battle, but try to make prayer your first action. You will be amazed at the answers you experience. Prayer is how we wage the battle: "The prayer of a righteous person is powerful and effective" (James 5:16b NIV).

Praying the Word of God will help you get started in the spiritual battle for your children and keep you on the right track. His Word always accomplishes His will. Isaiah 55:10–11 says, "As the rain and the snow come down from heaven, and do not return to it without watering the earth and making it bud and flourish, so that it yields seed for the sower and bread for the eater, so is my word that goes out from my mouth: It will not return to me empty, but will accomplish what I desire and achieve the purpose for which I sent it" (NIV).

Children's pastor, Noah Hutchison, posted the following scripture based prayers to pray over your children in his blog which can be found at http://noahhutchison.com/christian-living/scriptures-to-pray-over-your-children/. I had a similar list of prayers posted on my refrigerator for years and still pray this way for my children and grandchildren.

1. Ephesians 1:17-19

   Lord, give our children the Spirit of wisdom and revelation, and the knowledge of You. That the eyes of their hearts be enlightened that they will know the hope to which you have called them, the riches of Your glorious inheritance in the saints and His Incomparably great power for us who believe.

2. Ephesians 3: 17-19

   These children are rooted and established in love; we pray that they may have power with all the saints to grasp how wide and long and high and deep is the love of Christ towards them, and to know this love that surpasses knowledge, that they may be filled to the measure of the fullness of God.

3. Ephesians 5:1 and 21

   Our children will be imitators of God and live a life of love. They will submit to others out of reverence to Christ.

4. Ephesians 6:1-3

   Our children will obey their parents in the Lord. They will honor their father and mother so that it may go well with them and that they may enjoy long life on earth.

5. 1 Timothy 4:12

   No one will look down on our children because they are young, but they set an example for the believers in speech, in conduct, in love, in faith and in purity.

6. Psalm 103:2-5

   Thank you Lord that our children won't forget His benefits. You forgive all their sins and heal all their diseases. You redeem their lives from the pit, and crown them with love and compassion. You satisfy their souls with good things so that their youth is renewed like the eagles.

7. Psalm 1:1-3

   Our children do not walk in the counsel of the ungodly or stand in the path of sinners or sit in the seat of scoffers. But their delight is in the law of the Lord and on His law they meditate day and night. They are like the trees planted by the rivers of water, which yield their fruit in season and whose leaf will not whither, and whatever they do prospers.

8. Psalm 119:10-11

   Our children seek You with all their hearts; they will not stray from Your commands; they have hidden Your word in their hearts that they may not sin against you.

9. Psalm 91:9-16

   Our children have made the Most High their dwelling place. No harm will befall them; no disaster will come near their tents. For He will give His angles charge over them to guard them in all their ways. They will carry them so that our children do not dash their foot against a stone. They will tread upon the lion and the cobra; they will trample them underfoot. Because our children love You, You will deliver them. You will set them on high. They will call upon You and You will answer them. You will be with them in trouble. You will deliver them and honor them and with long life. You will satisfy them and show them Your salvation.

10. Acts 1:8, 2:38

Our children will receive the gift of the Holy Spirit. They will receive power when the Holy Spirit comes upon them.

11. Joel 2:28

Thank you Lord that it will come to pass that You will pour out Your Spirit on our children; our sons and daughters shall prophesy, dream dreams, and see visions.

12. 1John 4:4

Greater is He that is in our children the he that is in the world.

13. Isaiah 54:13-14 and 17

All our children shall be taught by the Lord and great will be their peace. In righteousness they will be established. Tyranny will be far from them; they will have nothing to fear. Terror will be far removed; it will not come near them. No weapon formed against them will prosper.

14. Mark 4:20

The hearts of our children are like good soil, they hear the word, accept it and produce a crop....100 times that which was sown.

15. 2 Timothy 2:22

Our children flee the evil desires of their youth and pursue righteousness, faith, love and peace, along with those who call on the Lord out of a pure heart.

Questions for Discussion

1. What are the most urgent prayers you have for your family right now?

2. Do you keep a prayer journal? If you do, you will see the progress your family is making and the intervention of God much more clearly. It will be an encouragement for you.

3. What is a prayer you have seen God answer in a powerful way?

4. How has prayer helped you cope, or how has it rejuvenated you?

5. Do you have a prayer life with the Lord now?

6. Do you know the loving nature of God? Describe His nature as it pertains to you.

7. Have you asked His forgiveness and received His salvation?

8. Is He Lord of your life? Talk about what this means to you.

Notes

Counting Noses

If it is Monday, I must have four children. Is it Monday?

As you already read, we raised a family of five children: his, mine, and ours. The revolving door was always in motion. Samantha was with us Wednesdays and every other weekend, as well as during other random times. Whitney and Cameron were with us most of the time, but not always. Stefan and Eric were with us all the time. Five noses.

For a while I had five children in five schools, each with a different schedule. I had one and a half hours from the time I dropped off the last child at school until I picked up the first child after school. During this limited period, I could grocery shop but not for anything that might perish in the sizzling Phoenix heat while I stopped to pick up child number four from kindergarten. No milk, no chicken, nothing frozen.

A separate grocery trip for ice cream was necessary, with no children along to slow my progress. I would dash from the grocer's freezer through the express check-out line and across the hot, semi-soft asphalt, grasp the car door handle with my hand wrapped in my shirt to protect its delicate digits from the searing metal, and pitch the ice cream tub to a location close to the air conditioner. Then I would weave my way through traffic and sprint through my entry to toss it into the freezer at home where it would be revived from its now semi-liquid state to a cone-worthy consistency once again. I share this example to illustrate my level of dedication to being a champion among moms. I'm sure it is no more than you would do.

I spent hours every day shuttling kids to and from school, activities, and sports. I learned the rules of their games, the quirks of community theater, the proper code of etiquette for depositing children at their various schools, and the right coat for a swimmer to wear when competing at outdoor pools during the winter. I carpooled, frequented swimming pools, and pooled the children together in an efficient manner. My most frequently worn accessory was a lanyard around my neck, from which dangled a laminated card listing players' names and jersey numbers. This enabled me to shout encouragement for the right child by name for every play of the game. "Run Forrest, run!"

Most parents go through something similar, but one thing that made it more of a challenge for me, with a blended family, was that I was always afraid I was missing someone. I had to think, every day, *Which kids do I have today?* I counted noses in the backseats, thinking, *Okay, I have Whitney today, but Cameron is at Dad's and Samantha is at Mom's. I have Stefan and Eric. Three noses—yep, all present and accounted for!"*

Meal planning was also a challenge. As I slaved away over dinner preparations—well, that's a bit of an exaggeration ... Sometimes, as I was boiling pasta and tearing lettuce for salad, Samantha would show up and say she was staying for four days. Okay, time to readjust. We would welcome her, and we would go to plan B or C or whatever it was for that day. No big deal. Remember that. It is no big deal to have extra noses unexpectedly; it is a gift of time to spend with them. Stretch the meal, add more bread, and set another place at the table. If you want the child to feel welcome, never make an ordeal out of his or her unexpected arrival or overextended stay. You wouldn't roll your eyes and sigh if your neighbor stopped by for a cup of coffee, would you? Give your stepchildren the same courtesy.

You and your loving spouse may have planned a really great night out, or in, without children. Maybe they were scheduled to be at their other parent's home for the weekend as spelled out in the visitation order. You might have been excited all week in anticipation of your precious time alone when the phone rang and your ex informed you that the kids couldn't come to his or her house for the weekend. Something came up, and it wasn't an excuse you viewed as important, but the fact was that he or she was not coming to get the kids, so your plans just went out the window. The way you respond to this disappointment will be an example to the children, either a good one or a bad one. If you complain, don't expect a pleasant weekend, much less the close relationship you desire with the children. If you adjust with grace, the children will be shown that they are valuable. Kids can enjoy a candlelit dinner and games by the fire too. Remember, you are training future spouses. Your example will travel through time to your grandchildren's lives.

Get used to this type of schedule, if you can call it a schedule, and you will be a lot happier. Rigidity will cause you to miss out on making the best of the unexpected times together. It's fine to have a parenting plan with a schedule, but be prepared for the inevitable schedule changes. Remember, several parents are involved in executing this schedule, and any number of problems may arise. That's life in the blended, not shaken, family.

Questions for Discussion

1. Discuss a time when your plans were interrupted because of something that happened in the children's other home.

2. What had to be sacrificed because of the interruption?

3. How did your family handle it?

4. How did your family benefit from the experience?

5. Could this situation be avoided in the future? If so, how?

6. Examine your heart. Have you worked through it, forgiven, and moved on?

Notes

That's Not Fair

One struggle common to blended families is that of fairness. Why is this issue such a common one and so difficult to maneuver? In an intact family the same two parents raise each child. However, not being static, life presents different options and opportunities to each person, even in the intact family.

Think about a nuclear, intact family. Is everything even? When one child gets new cleats, do all the children get cleats? What if they don't need cleats? If one child goes to a movie with a friend, would all the children have to go along? No, they would not. Things are not perfectly even in the intact family. However, over time things probably even out to some extent. The family goes through a progression of growth or ups and downs together and no one feels guilty about being unfair.

Let's say that Jeff and Ashley have their first child. They are in their twenties, barely making ends meet. They love their child, and the child gets Jeff and Ashley's attention all to himself. He goes to a caring daycare facility, the family never takes vacations, birthdays are simple functions at home, and the child and parents are happy.

When the next child comes along, Jeff and Ashley are just starting their careers. They love both children, their attention is divided between them, and they have a little more money to spend. This child has less individual time with the parents but goes to a nicer daycare facility than the first child did as a toddler. The family can now afford to vacation by camping in the nearby mountains and to have large birthday parties at the local kids' play center.

A few years later a third child is born into the family. Now in well-established careers, the parents are able to afford vacations in Hawaii, ski days for the children's birthdays, and top-notch educations. They love the children, and everyone is happy. They have gone through a progression of growth, and no one feels guilty about what one child got compared to another. The progression in other intact families may not be as dramatic and may in fact go the other way financially. However, the intact family is in it together, which is what I intended to illustrate here.

In a blended family the dynamics are much different. The parents in the two families who are raising a child may have completely different budgets, be in different phases in their life earnings, and have completely opposing ideas about what is appropriate to provide for their children. Different families provide different opportunities and material possessions. Parents try to be fair, but the balancing act requires too many plates to be spinning.

Our two girls are only eighteen months apart in age, stepsisters who love each other and are, to this day, best friends. When they were little, I overheard a conversation between them. What I heard began with Whitney saying something like, "You know when your dress gets too short and you have to wear shorts under it?" Samantha's look of bewilderment made her reply unnecessary: "No, what are you talking about?" She had never needed to make her dresses last beyond their appropriate length. She was the only child and only grandchild in her other family, and she always had new clothes before she outgrew the old ones. That's not really fair.

Have you ever watched your children's faces glow with glee on the "It's a Small World" ride five times in one day at Disneyland? It's the happiest place on earth. Top their noggins with mouse ears, fill their fists with lollypops, and it's a wonder to behold. After a day of wonder, you ride the monorail back to the hotel for a rest.

Have you ever watched your children play a game of lava? Outside of the food bank there are some broken concrete parking blocks. This game is especially realistic when you can see the heat waves rise from the parking lot. The object of the game is to step across the whole line of broken, wobbly parking blocks without slipping onto the asphalt, a.k.a. the "lava." The children squeal in make-believe torment as they imagine the earth shaking and as they flee the flowing, molten rock. There are usually a hero and a damsel in distress acting out their roles. Inside the food bank, once your food bag has been filled, you take it and your heroes and damsels across the lava to your minivan where the kids buckle up for the ride home.

What if your children play lava at the food bank, and your husband's children go to Disneyland? That's totally not fair.

If the parents in one household give evenly to all their children and stepchildren, inequity may still exist in the children's lives because of the vast differences in their other families. The parents created this mess by divorcing, so they may feel guilty and try to compensate by buying things or doing things that they cannot afford in order to keep up with the competition.

If children growing up in two homes compare what they are given in terms of opportunities and material possessions, they will find that it's not fair. That is just a fact of life for these kids. This type of childhood is actually more like the real world experience they will face in adulthood. Inequity is everywhere.

How should this touchy subject be handled? Christmas is a time when the unfairness seems to be magnified. It presents the most obvious inequity because the gifts are opened by all the children on the same day. Do your children know exactly how many of the presents under the Christmas tree are for them? I never taught my kids to count their awaiting gifts. They did it on their own—they compared. As a child in my intact family I never counted the gifts under my Christmas tree. There must have been some thought of unfairness in our kids' minds that caused them to compare the number of gifts they were to receive.

Every Christmas Eve when the kids were young, we had a large family gathering with my extended family. Then we went to church together. On Christmas morning we read the story of Christ's birth in the Bible over cinnamon rolls and eggnog, and then we opened gifts with our children.

In the early afternoon our ping-pong kids went to their other parents' houses. Samantha would get loads of other gifts—, hundreds, I think. Although I didn't count, she did. Cameron and Whitney would get a load as well, but not as many. For our boys who had no other parents, the gift getting was over before the big kids left for their other Christmas celebrations. If the gifts are the most important focus of Christmas, receiving far fewer gifts than the other kids can be a real disappointment.

You have heard the expression: "Christians live as if it is Christmas all year long." The gift of the birth of Christ lives in our hearts all year. In a blended family this expression takes on a whole new meaning. The unbalanced receiving of stuff and experiences also lasts all year, every year. Your "one-home" children may not appreciate the fact that they have both parents living with them all the time, when the wrapped gifts for their sister number 127, their brother gets fifty-eight, and they get twelve, including the stocking stuffers.

Teaching these kids to appreciate the finer things, the more spiritual aspects of Christmas, and their lives in general, is more of a challenge when the mountain of tangible evidence is that someone in their family who lives in their house is getting much more.

Trying to keep up or adjust to the other family's way of life is not going to work at Christmas or any time. You, as a parent, need to know that you cannot make things even. Confidently model grace for them by showing happiness for another's good fortune. Let them express themselves, and validate their feelings.

In your day-to-day life, you will also make decisions that make things apparently unfair. Explain your position to the children. For instance, "Our family requires the children to earn their own money to buy a car or pay for their own entertainment in order for them to develop a sense of responsibility, and we help you with that by giving you an allowance." Or perhaps you need to explain the opposite: "Our family thinks that our college students should be given a car so that they can come home on the weekends." Neither is wrong; they are just different positions, both valid.

It may be hard for the children to grasp, but it is what it is, and it is okay.

Questions for Discussion

1. Does it bother you if things are not perfectly even between what your children have and what your stepchildren have?

2. Does it bother them?

3. Do your children say, "That's not fair! He gets to ..., so why can't I?"

4. Do you struggle to make things fair for your children and stepchildren?

5. The most obvious inequity presents itself on Christmas because all the children open gifts on the same day. Do your children notice? How do they respond if there is a big difference? How do you respond?

6. Do you and your spouse differ in your ideas about what to provide and what to have your children earn for themselves?

7. Do you have open communication with your ex with regard to inequities?

8. Is there a compromise you can implement in order to make things fairer? Is that important to you?

Notes

It's the Most Wonderful Time of the Year—or Is It?

after "A Visit from St. Nicholas"
(a.k.a. "'Twas the Night Before Christmas")
by Clement Clarke Moore

The children were nestled all snug in their beds,
while visions of sugarplums danced in their heads.
Mama in her house, with me in my condo,
had us a battle on the scale of Rambo.
With the phone to my ear, there arose such a clatter.
Kids sprang from their beds to see what was the matter.
I paced and I fumed and I let out a shout:
"You must let me have them!" and Mama did pout.
The kids at my house with tear-streaked little faces
asked if their mama had gifts in their places.
Away to the window I flew like a flash,
Threw the phone to the sidewalk, and heard it land with a crash.
The moon lit the yard, and I saw it in pieces.
My head hung in shame, and my face formed deep creases.
The tears then did flow, and I thought, *What a mess.*
Did I ask for this when at the altar said yes?

> Since that day full of hope, things had fallen apart.
> I, with kids in tow, had to make a fresh start.
> The stockings were hung. The kids' hearts had been light.
> But I ruined their sleep on Christmas Eve night.

Holiday mix-ups are more emotionally charged than mix-ups about regular weekend visits. Most of us have more activities, guests, and expectations surrounding the holidays. Our family traditions may be in conflict with the children's other family's traditions. We want it to be so nice and fun. All of these things tend to add stress, which is exactly what we don't want for these special times of year.

You probably have a court order regarding holidays, but it may make things go more smoothly if you discuss in detail the exact plans, times, and dates with the kids' other families. A casual chat with your ex-spouse about your Christmas plans is likely to be forgotten or muddled in the busyness of the holiday festivities. That is when trouble erupts. Get plans on the calendar, and if necessary, email the plans to your ex-spouse so that there is no confusion. Having everything in writing for both of you to reference will help ensure a smoother holiday season.

Holiday visitation is not the only discussion to be had. Here are some things you may want to discuss with the ex and his family ahead of time:

- Gifts the children will receive
- Gifts the children will give others
- Budget for the children to shop for gifts
- Clothes they need for events over the holidays
- Haircuts
- Family photos
- Diet restrictions
- Schoolwork or reading that needs to be done over the holiday

Plan and communicate as far in advance as possible. Figure out what works for your family. You may decide to alternate holidays and switch them the next year. The children might spend part of the holiday in each home.

Our ping-pong kids, Cameron, Whitney, and Samantha, went to their other parents' homes for Thanksgiving weekend every year. Our two boys, Stefan and Eric, stayed with Steve and me. As I said in the previous chapter, we had all five children on Christmas Eve and for Christmas morning, and at one o'clock Christmas afternoon Cameron, Whitney, and Samantha went to their other parents' homes. Stefan and Eric stayed with us and spent time with our shared family and friends. It worked for us, and because the schedule was the same every year, the kids knew what to expect and traditions were consistent.

In 2012 we spent the first Thanksgiving ever with Samantha. She was twenty-seven years old, married, and a mother of one small boy. As usual, we made the trek to our cabin in Flagstaff, Arizona, for our annual feast and family gathering. We used to drive two hours from Phoenix, but in 2012, as we do now, we made the long trip from Colorado Springs. Thirty-one humans and eleven of our canine family members converged on the cabin with side dishes and desserts in hand—that is, those of us with opposable thumbs and not paws. The turkeys waited with the early arrivals. We all look forward to this trip every year, and in 2012, finally, on her twenty-seventh birthday, Samantha was a part of it with her husband, son, and English mastiff in tow. It had been a long wait to have her with us for Thanksgiving. The time had arrived, and I was delighted.

With numerous holidays every year, planning and bargaining for time with the kids can be trying. If you are the mom, it seems logical for you to get your kids for Mother's Day, but if you are the stepmom, don't count on it, even if you have primary custody of the children. Look on the bright side; if you don't have the kids for New Year's Day, maybe you can start a new Groundhog Day family tradition.

Communicate and plan ahead to have merry Christmases and happy holidays every year.

Questions for Discussion

1. Do you have expectations for Christmas, Thanksgiving, Easter, etc. that you assume your ex-spouse knows about?

2. Have you discussed the plans in detail with him or her?

3. Is there an unresolved conflict regarding the holiday visitation plan?

4. What can you do to make things go more smoothly for your children?

5. Can you be flexible with some of your family traditions?

6. Will it be easy to discuss the plans with your ex?

7. Will you help your child buy or make a gift for your ex, his or her spouse, or their children?

8. Will you help your stepchild buy or make a gift for your spouse's ex, his or her spouse, or their children?

9. What have you already accomplished toward a smooth and happy holiday for your children and stepchildren?

10. Can you envision a time in the future when you will have all your children together for a holiday that you currently have to let them celebrate elsewhere?

Notes

A Picture-Perfect Family

I like Facebook. I like to share photos with my out-of-town family and see new baby pictures posted by friends far away. I originally set up a Facebook account to keep in touch with a friend who moved to South Korea with her husband who was stationed overseas with the military for three years. This was an easy and free method that enabled them to keep in touch with their friends—real friends—back in the states. It was great to see them in their surroundings on outings in South Korea. I even learned some things about the culture, cuisine, and geography of South Korea from their Facebook posts. This is online social networking at its finest.

However, when used incorrectly, Facebook communication replaces real face-to-face communication for many people. Platitudes replace enduring encouragement that can only be achieved in longer conversations, in person. Parentheses replace hugs. Facebook friends fill a void with a perceived relationship crafted by succinct writers portraying themselves as your "besties."

Carried to the extreme, Facebook becomes a type of therapist—and not a very good one. Airing dirty laundry online may get you some sympathy comments, but does it really help you work through issues? Working out your feelings in this highly public forum is not likely to benefit you or anyone involved. Find trustworthy people you can talk to in person. Get a real hug from someone who cares about you instead of "()."

Facebook is not your therapist. No one is asking a therapist's questions. No one will ask you the deep questions that will help you work through the painful issues you may be experiencing.

That being said, as parents you would be wise to watch out for troubling posts or comments from your children. If you do see comments from your children, you are the person who is close by and can help them work through their emotions and trauma face to face. Facebook certainly has its place and can be used for good. I know of a teen who was living through a trying period and communicating about it through poetry on Facebook. His concerned siblings all talked to their parents about it. His parents had not seen the post because the teen had blocked them from it, but they knew that something was wrong. This bit of information enabled them to be better informed in order to help their child, and the outcome has been very positive.

When Facebook is used as a therapist, personal problems are aired to a good chunk of the loosely connected public as if on stage in an arena. Here is how I see it. If you have an issue with your spouse and post your grievance on Facebook, everyone sees it. Later you work out your differences with your spouse, forgive him or her, and continue in your fabulous marriage.

Back in the days before the existence of the Internet you might have mentioned a personal problem to your neighbor, in confidence, and heard her perspective on the subject. She might have helped you work through the issue. On Facebook all confidentiality is lost. This is the difference between telling and broadcasting. Everyone who sees that post now has a preconceived, negative perception about your spouse. Like it or not, people are talking about him or her and this issue, and they may not be as willing to forgive your spouse as you are. They don't have the investment in the relationship that you have. Moving forward, there will be a hurdle to jump every time you see these people, the Facebook friends and possibly friends of friends, and so on, who saw your post. It makes things harder on your marriage.

Facebook posts rarely say, "Thank you for your comment on my dilemma. It has been a life-changing realization for me to hear that from you, and I realize now what the underlying problem was." What I have seen is that people who post their problems resolve nothing, at least not there in the arena. I can only hope that they are working off camera, so to speak, and that when their next post says, "Look at my beautiful garden," the aforementioned issue has been resolved. I doubt it.

Replacing wise counsel with Facebook blasts of communication lacks the advantage of developing problem-solving skills. Although some people post timely quips and fresh ideas that amuse me, many others don't put a lot of thought into their status updates. The ensuing comments might receive a quick glance, and the original poster of the comment might feel justified or even momentarily comforted. But then what? Nothing replaces time spent in the physical presence of people who can really communicate thoughtfully and help you solve problems, make you think deeply, and pray with you.

A lot has been said here about the effects of negative Facebook posts. Consider this on the flip side. Not every post you see on Facebook paints an accurate picture of what a family is going through. Would you send out a Christmas card photo that portrays your family at its worst: sad, angry, and disheveled? Not a chance. Likewise, many people only post the best of everything on Facebook. I like my profile picture taken in flattering light rather than when the sun streaks its harsh rays across my facial creases. The shadows age me to appear, well, my current age. Be honest—don't you do this, too? Therefore, don't get all bummed out about your hard life because of the flowery speech and lovely photos of other families laughing as they run through fields of sunshine, hand in hand, wearing cute color-coordinated outfits in the latest styles. Their kids throw up, throw tantrums, and throw their mothers into a tizzy, too. They wake up cranky, and they have bad days, bad breath, and bad manners at times as well. Nobody's life is that perfect, so don't endanger your family's unity by comparing it to an inaccurate profile on Facebook. Don't compare your everyday life to someone's Facebook highlights.

Google "Facebook-caused depression" and you will see a plethora of articles debating the theory that online social networking causes depression or jealousy. Some experts say that online social networking causes depression, and some say that depressed people tend to be online more than people who are not depressed. Just be aware that if your online social networking habits tend to make you feel bad about your family or give you a negative outlook on life, it is time to take a break. Otherwise, go ahead and post your photos and share comments. Just don't get too caught up in the bombardment of drama offered there. Keep your family's best interests and protection in the forefront, always. Your family is not available for public consumption.

Questions for Discussion

1. Do you rely upon online social networking to fill a void in your life?

2. Are your children or stepchildren replacing real social interaction with online "friendships"?

3. Have you checked your children's and stepchildren's Facebook statuses? If so, are they posting anything that could be a sign of trouble?

4. Have you been alerted to any family issues online? If so, have you addressed those issues in person?

5. Do you need to step away from your computer and draw closer to God and your family?

6. Why do you think people vent their problems online for all to see?

7. How can you help people who post issues to work through their difficulties?

8. Do you struggle with an Internet addiction?

9. How does online social networking negatively impact your blended family?

10. How does online social networking negatively impact your attitude?

11. How does online social networking positively impact your life?

Notes

Extreme Circumstances

Following is quotation by a twenty-something-year-old young woman who grew up in a blended family:

> "Unless you are a terrible person who shouldn't be involved in your daughter's life due to extreme circumstances (you're a murderer, you have un-fatherly affection for her, etc.) ... you're just looking for an excuse to satisfy your own desire for freedom and space. You made 'em (your children); stick with 'em!
>
> ★sigh★ I'd make a terrible counselor.
>
> Not everyone is divorcing because of an "extreme circumstance"; most people divorce because they're selfish. Sure, there are a lot of other factors and feelings that play into it, but the bottom line is selfishness. Their personal comfort becomes their idol so they choose comfort over the work it would take to fix the marriage/family ... "I just don't feel the sparks anymore" isn't extreme enough."

This woman's biological father was absent for most of her life. That's her view on the subject of divorce. What do you think? Are your reasons for breaking up the family legitimate or are they selfish?

There is nothing funny in this chapter. As much as I realize the value of a sense of humor in hard circumstances, or of seeing things in a positive light, there is nothing positive about domestic violence. If your spouse is doing things that are dangerous, take the kids to safety and get help. Things may turn around, but I don't want you or your children to end up dead. Get out quickly, and then reach out to a trusted friend, your family, a church, and/or law enforcement. There are places to go in your community to get help. Do a web search for battered women's or men's shelters, domestic violence help, or abuse shelters in your area. Never keep it to yourself, hoping that things will get better.

In some cases you might need to rely on programs that will help you escape a dangerous situation. The Address Confidentiality Program (ACP) provides relocated survivors of domestic violence, sexual offenses, or stalking, with a substitute address to use in place of their actual address when they apply for or receive state or local government services (i.e. driver's license, voter registration, public school records). The goal of the ACP is to prevent an abuser or potential abuser from finding the survivor through the state's public records. The ACP is a records protection program, not a witness protection program. The ACP does not assist participants with legal advice, obtaining new names, or obtaining new social security numbers, and it does not help with relocating to a new residence. Contact your state about this program.

That said, take an honest look at yourself and your circumstances. If you are contemplating leaving your marriage, be sure that it is truly in the children's best interest. If you have people in your life who give you marriage advice to "get out and get healthy," analyze that advice in light of Scripture. I will list Scripture references later.

Boredom is not grounds for divorce, nor is a difference in parenting styles or differing personal interests. If you didn't address these things before marriage, hang onto what brought you together in the first place, and do something for yourself to ward off the boredom. Everyone gets bored at times. Do you think your little children care if you are bored? No. They do not. They usually love both of their parents and thrive on the stability of their parents' marriage.

I dealt with a lot of guilt in ending my first marriage. For years I tried to keep the marriage intact. Women in the church advised me to "love him into the kingdom," and they told me, "God hates divorce." I realize that I am treading on grounds for theological debate here. God does hate divorce. He also hates hardness of hearts, adultery, and abuse or mistreatment of wives, husbands, and children. All of these things factor into making the decision to divorce, and no two situations are exactly the same. Carefully weigh your options.

Malachi 2:13–16 states,

> Another thing you do: You flood the LORD's altar with tears. You weep and wail because he no longer looks with favor on your offerings or accepts them with pleasure from your hands. You ask, "Why?" It is because the LORD is the witness between you and the wife of your youth. You have been unfaithful to her, though she is your partner, the wife of your marriage covenant. Has not the one God made you? You belong to him in body and spirit. And what does the one God seek? Godly offspring. So be on your guard, and do not be unfaithful to the wife of your youth. "The man who hates and divorces his wife," says the LORD, the God of Israel, "does violence to the one he should protect," says the LORD Almighty. So be on your guard, and do not be unfaithful. (NIV)

I believe that if there were true repentance, it would be better to forgive past indiscretions and save the marriage. I know people who have been able to work through difficult times, including infidelity, and have been able to prosper as a married couple.

Dr. Laura Slessinger, a psychologist and marriage counselor, tells callers to her radio program that there are three A's that are reasons for divorce: adultery, abuse, and addiction. For your safety and the safety of the children, you might be wise to distance yourself from your spouse if you are dealing with these things in your marriage.

I grieved the loss of my first love and my dreams. It saddens me that my children's home was broken. I loved my husband, but there were irreconcilable differences that made the marriage impossible. I am forever grateful for the restored life God has given me. I know that I live in the forgiveness of my Savior and that my current marriage to Steve is blessed.

Marriage is a covenant created by God. We vow at the altar to stay married until death do us part. There are many Scriptures that address circumstances of divorce and remarriage. I want to clarify that neither divorce nor remarriage is required when these circumstances exist, but sometimes divorce becomes necessary because of these circumstances.

Remarriage is obviously permitted if you are widowed: "A woman is bound to her husband as long as he lives. But if her husband dies, she is free to marry anyone she wishes, but he must belong to the Lord" (1 Corinthians 7:39 NIV). Scripture also says, "By law a married woman is bound to her husband as long as he is alive, but if her husband dies, she is released from the law that binds her to him. So then, if she has sexual relations with another man while her husband is still alive, she is called an adulteress. But if her husband dies, she is released from that law and is not an adulteress if she marries another man" (Romans 7:2–3 NIV).

In fact, in biblical times a widow was to be married by her husband's brother in order to be cared for and to carry on the family name. Deuteronomy 25:5 says, "If brothers are living together and one of them dies without a son, his widow must not marry outside the family. Her husband's brother shall take her and marry her and fulfill the duty of a brother-in-law to her." Although this is not our cultural norm in the United States today, it further shows that remarriage is okay for widows and widowers.

Scripture also says,

> To the married I give this command (not I, but the Lord): A wife must not separate from her husband. But if she does, she must remain unmarried or else be reconciled to her husband. And a husband must not divorce his wife. To the rest I say this (I, not the Lord): If any brother has a wife who is not a believer and she is willing to live with him, he must not divorce her. And if a woman has a husband who is not a believer and he is willing to live with her, she must not divorce him. For the unbelieving husband has been sanctified through his wife, and the unbelieving wife has been sanctified through her believing husband. Otherwise your children would be unclean, but as it is, they are holy. But if the unbeliever leaves, let it be so. The brother or the sister is not bound in such circumstances; God has called us to live in peace. (1 Corinthians 7:10–15 NIV)

It appears at first glance that once divorced, you should not remarry. Take it to the Lord in prayer, and realize that divorce and remarriage are not decisions to be taken lightly. However, read again verse 15, where it says that the one who has been left is not bound. The person is free to remarry. This violates the original plan that marriage would be permanent and a reflection of the relationship of Christ with the church, but there is more to the story: "If we confess our sins, He is faithful and just to forgive us our sins" (1 John 1:9).

Revisit the story of the woman caught in adultery as told in John 8:4–11. She was caught in the act and brought to Jesus. Those who brought her before the Lord said, "Now in the Law, Moses commanded us to stone such women; what then do you say?" Jesus answered them by saying, "He who is without sin among you, let him be the first to throw a stone at her." Her accusers, realizing their own sin, left. Jesus said, "Woman, where are they? Did no one condemn you?" And she said, "No one, Lord." And Jesus said, "Neither do I condemn you; go your own way. From now on sin no more."

This is the covenant of forgiveness we live under; this is the good news and the reason Jesus came. Further, Psalm 103:8–12 says, "The LORD is compassionate and gracious, slow to anger, abounding in love. He will not always accuse, nor will He harbor his anger forever; He does not treat us as our sins deserve or repay us according to our iniquities. For as high as the heavens are above the earth, so great is His love for those who fear Him; as far as the east is from the west, so far has He removed our transgressions from us" (NIV). Praise God for that!

Questions for Discussion:

1. If there are circumstances in your marriage that leave you with divorce as the only option, you are free. Considering what you have just read, what is your best option at this point?

2. If you have been remarried and are wondering where you stand in the sight of God, you are loved and forgiven. Do you accept the forgiveness of the Lord?

3. Are you and your children safe in your home, or are you in danger of harm?

4. What will you do if you or your children are not safe?

5. What do you understand as grounds for divorce?

6. Can you back that up in Scripture?

7. Is your spouse in an adulterous relationship?

8. Are you bored in your marriage?

9. What do you do in your life to ward off boredom with or apart from your spouse?

10. Have you developed personal interests in your own life?

11. Are you looking for an out in you marriage?

12. Do you see how God has redeemed you in your current marriage? Describe His redemption.

13. Do you realize the freedom you have in Christ if you need a new beginning?

14. How does freedom make you feel?

15. What will you do because of your freedom?

Notes

A Redeemed Life

Trust in the LORD with all your heart and lean not on your own understanding; in all your ways submit to him, and he will make your paths straight.

—Proverbs 3:5–6 NIV

You are in your stepchildren's lives for a purpose. Your blended family was not unforeseen by God. You may be very surprised by it, but He is not. You are not called to be a superhero stepparent but to tap into the supernatural power of the living God. Trust in Him. Do not lean on your own understanding. Acknowledge Him. Submit to Him. Then the broken pieces of your life and your heart will be made whole again in Jesus. What the Enemy means for evil will be made to work for good by the God who made you.

Start by giving Him what little you have, and watch Him perform miracles in your family. There was a time when I felt I was too broken to do any good for anyone. I sobbed multiple times. I am not a pretty crier. I was sad and puffy eyed and snotty. There were times I could hardly catch my breath because I was so grief-stricken about what my life had become. I had suffered at the hands of others and because of my own poor choices. I saw no redemption for my life, even though I was already saved. I knew that the God who created the heavens and the earth forgave me, but I could not forgive myself. I thought that I could not be used by God to do any good on this planet. But His word says in Jeremiah 29:11, "'For I know the plans I have for you,' declares the LORD, 'plans to prosper you and not to harm you, plans to give you hope and a future.'" I had to believe that, so I persevered in prayer.

In a vision I stood in the ocean and saw huge waves crashing toward me. I felt as if I was being dragged underwater. Every time I tried to stand and just felt the sandy ocean floor with my toes, another wave knocked me off of my feet and filled my gasping mouth with another salty surge. Repeatedly I was knocked down by waves that came from different angles in rapid succession. I stood back up, gasping for air, for life, seeing no way to save myself. I cried out for God, and He clearly spoke these words to me: "Reach inside yourself." I reached my hand into the empty cavity that was me. I saw my hand reaching down deep. "Go deeper," He said, and I did. My groping hand reached to the bottom of the vessel of my soul, and my elbow bumped against my heart as I swirled my hand around in complete darkness. I fell asleep still searching for the inner strength to move forward in my life and ministry. When I awoke the next morning, my hand was still searching, but it was coming up empty, my elbow still bumping my heart.

I said to God, "There is nothing here but my heart." In my mind's eye I saw His hand beckon, "Give it to me."

"But it is broken," I replied. I saw Him smile and beckon again. It was then that I realized that God was going to use my broken heart and His strength to accomplish His purpose in my life and to help other people. The result of being willing to give my broken heart to the Lord is a redeemed life. It is my redeemed life. It has been multiplied in my family and in the lives of strangers. My broken pieces were gathered up and made whole again, supernaturally. The same God who did that for me will do it for you.

Whatever you have done, whatever your story, you can break the cycle of destruction in your life and become what God intends for you to be for yourself, your family, and your community. Just be willing, and give God what little you have. Start now.

When my sister said to me, "It's like you have a new life," my response was, "I do." God made all things new in me when I submitted to His lordship. There is no better thing you can do; there is no better way to become the parent and stepparent you want to be for those precious children in your care. You can choose how you want to live your new life: in victory or as a victim, with joy or in pain, trying to do everything by your own strength and brains or relying on the strength and wisdom of God, who created the universe and knew you before you were born.

In the past you might have been a victim of terrible circumstances or a terrible person. If this is still happening, get out and get help. If not, leave its memory behind and live in the fullness of joy that Christ gives. He created you; He can surely fix you. Ask for His healing and act on it, even if you don't feel completely over your past wounds. Allow the Holy Spirit to work in your heart, and move on and into the abundant life Jesus came to give you.

There is no doubt in my mind that you hurt because of wounds you suffered in your past. I suffered myself and am no stranger to emotional and spiritual pain. Your recovery may be even more painful than the initial wound. It hurts. It is real. It requires fixing, not denial. Fixing anything requires work, whether it is a bike, a car, a window, or your emotions and spirit.

I injured my back at work. It's not a dramatic injury story, such as "I fell from the rock face of a huge mountain" or "I landed wrong while performing a fantastic gymnastic trick." I was lifting a tray of sandwiches, and my back just went out. It really hurt. I felt stabbing pain and had trouble standing up. My mind raced: *What just happened? This did not just happen. How long will this last? The pain has to go away now. Will I ever be able to stand? What should I do now? Who should I call?*

I was in bed for days and then in physical therapy for about a month. I started to get used to the pain and to adjust to moderate activity. At physical therapy I feared a relapse every time I lifted the weighted wooden box and carried it across the room because I felt a twinge of pain. Sometimes I feared even the possibility of feeling a twinge of pain. But the therapist was right when he said that the pain I felt was not a new injury and to keep going. He said I might feel pain between therapy sessions too and not to worry about it. I was not reinjuring my back. My muscles strengthened, and I learned new techniques for lifting so that I wouldn't hurt my back again. I gradually felt better. Each time I went to therapy, I could see that I was closer to full recovery, and that made me happy and hopeful.

Just as physical therapy is often a painful experience requiring your dedication and hard work, the recovery of those emotional and spiritual wounds may be painful, requiring your dedication and hard work. But let the healing take place. Do not stand in the way of it. The time for denial is over. Go to Jesus in prayer repeatedly. As you go, you will be strengthened in your inner being. You will learn new techniques for life, parenting, and loving as He loves you. You might fear relapse when you feel that twinge of a painful memory that comes to mind, but remember, that memory is in the past and is not a new injury. Keep on going to Jesus and trust that He will lead you well to wholeness and full recovery. When you begin to see His love and your progress, it will make you happy and hopeful. You can have a whole new life. He did it for me, and He will do it for you.

Your blended family will benefit from your wholeness. As you grow in the love of the Lord, you will pour out love to those around you, your spouse, your children, and your stepchildren.

This book has given you stories from my life and ideas to help you out as you raise your blended family, but the most important thing that I hope you grasp is that God loves you, He has a plan for you, and it is a plan for good and not for evil. He will guide you on your journey toward having a family that is blended, not shaken.

Questions for Discussion

1. What are some of the reasons that God put you into the lives of your stepchildren?

2. What are some reasons God put your stepchildren into your life?

3. Have your family relationships improved recently? If so or if not, explain.

4. Where will you go from here to improve your blended family relationships?

5. What emotional and/or spiritual wounds do you need to deal with to be healed and healthy?

6. What gives you hope for the future?

7. How have you experienced God's love in your life? In what ways?

8. Have you moved on, or are you still living as a victim of your past pain?

9. If you have moved on, what are some things you did to help in the process? What have you moved on to?

10. If you are still living as a victim, what can you do to start the healing process? What is holding you back?

11. Have you given broken pieces of yourself to God? If so, share what happened.

12. What broken pieces can you give to God today?

13. Can you rely on God's strength and go through necessary therapy either alone with Him, with your spouse, or with a counselor?

14. What are your dreams for the future? What are your dreams for next month, next year, five years, and ten years from now? What about in your older age when the children are grown and gone?

15. List the goals that will help you realize your dreams.

Salvation Prayer

Is Jesus your Lord and Savior? If not, would you be willing to give Him a chance? He already loves you and is waiting for you. John 3:16 says, "For God so loved the world that he gave his one and only Son, that whoever believes in him shall not perish but have eternal life" (NIV).

When you believe in Him as your Savior, not only are you saved, but also Jesus says that He came so that you will have an abundant life. John 10:10 says, "The thief comes only to steal and kill and destroy; I have come that they may have life, and have it to the full" (NIV).

If you have not done so already and would like to live in the fullness that Jesus promises, believe in Him and pray this prayer: "Lord Jesus, I confess that I am a sinner. I ask You to come into my life and forgive me of all my sins. I want to follow You all my life.

Thank You for saving me. I believe with my heart and I confess with my mouth that You are my Lord and Savior. I pray this in Your name, Jesus. Amen."

Find a Christian to share your salvation experience with and a local church to plug into. You are on your way, and I couldn't be happier for you.

Notes

Notes

1. Ron Deal, "Marriage, Family, and Stepfamily Statistics: Spotlight Statistics," *SmartStepfamilies,* last modified April 2014, http://www.smartstepfamilies.com/view/statistics.
2. Karney, Garvan, and Thomas (2003).
3. Wendy Manning (National Center for Family and Marriage Research), personal communication, January 2010.
4. Parker (2011).
5. United States Census (2007).
6. Manning, personal communication.
7. United States Bureau of the Census (2006).
8. Cherlin (2009).
9. Gary D. Chapman, *The Five Love Languages: The Secret to Love That Lasts* (Chicago: Northfield Publishing, 2010).

www.ingramcontent.com/pod-product-compliance
Lightning Source LLC
LaVergne TN
LVHW051950060526
838201LV00059B/3585